HOMEMADE HEALTHY
DOG FOOD COOKBOOK

180+ Easy Recipes for Nutritious, Home-Cooked Meals.
The Ultimate Healthy Guide for Furry Family Members

Geri MacLean

The information in this book is intended for educational purposes only and should not be construed as veterinary advice. The recipes and dietary recommendations are designed to offer general guidelines for preparing homemade dog food. Every dog is unique, and individual nutritional requirements can vary based on age, breed, health status, and activity level.

When considering new food or recipes for your dog, it's essential to consult with your veterinarian. They can provide personalized advice, ensuring the recipes suit your dog's specific needs and health conditions. Please note that the author and publisher are not liable for any adverse effects or consequences of using the recipes or information in this book.

The nutritional information provided for each recipe is a standard calculation and may vary based on the specific ingredients and preparation methods. It's important to regularly monitor your dog's health and well-being and adjust their diet as necessary. This should always be done under the guidance of a qualified veterinary professional.

By using the recipes and information in this book, you acknowledge that you are doing so at your own risk and that the author and publisher are not liable for any outcomes of using this information. Always prioritize your dog's health and consult with a veterinarian to ensure the best care and nutrition for your pet.

Hi, Dear Dog Parent!

My journey into homemade dog food began not out of curiosity but necessity. My Golden Retrievers, Max and Daisy, started experiencing health problems I couldn't solve with commercial dog food. It led me to take a closer look at what they were eating. The more I researched, the clearer it became: I had to take matters into my own hands.

Creating homemade meals for Max and Daisy was about more than just solving their health issues. It was also the beginning of an extensive research project. I worked closely with veterinarians and spent countless hours experimenting in the kitchen. This book is the result of thorough research and several years of trial and error in finding the perfect balance of nutrients for my dogs.

As Max and Daisy's health improved, friends and neighbors started noticing and asking for advice. Before long, I was helping others navigate the world of homemade dog food. My kitchen became a hub for recipe swaps and nutritional consultations. This word-of-mouth expertise eventually earned me a reputation as a trusted advisor in the local dog breeding community. Writing this book was a natural next step, a way to compile and share everything I've learned.

Thank you for choosing my book. I sincerely appreciate it. I hope you'll find answers to all your questions here. Scan the QR code to share your thoughts on the Homemade Healthy Dog Food Cookbook. Your feedback helps fellow dog parents!

You may have noticed that this cookbook doesn't include recipe pictures. I made this decision to keep the book affordable for everyone. But don't worry! Turn to the last page for a unique gift waiting just for you!

Happy reading,
Geri MacLean

Contents

THE IMPORTANCE OF HOMEMADE DOG FOOD

When I was a girl growing up on a farm in North Carolina, everything was homemade. From the bread on our table to the jams in our pantry, we valued knowing what went into our food. The same principle applies to what we feed our furry friends. My two golden retrievers, Max and Daisy, thrive on the homemade meals I prepare for them, and I want to share why this approach is also worth considering for your dogs.

First, let's talk about control. When you make your dog's food at home, you decide on every ingredient that goes into their bowl, ensuring they get the highest quality nutrition without any dubious additives. Store-bought dog food often contains ingredients you need help to pronounce or understand.

Nutrition is the key to good health, and our pets benefit from fresh, wholesome ingredients just as much as we do. Since I started cooking for them, Max and Daisy's coats have been shinier, their eyes brighter, and their energy levels have increased. It's not rocket science but good, old-fashioned common sense.

Moreover, homemade dog food allows you to tailor meals to your dog's dietary needs. Max, for example, has a sensitive stomach and doesn't do well with certain grains. Daisy, on the other hand, has a bit of a weight problem (but don't tell her I said that!). By preparing their meals, I can ensure Max gets a grain-free diet while keeping Daisy's calorie intake in check.

Now, let's address the elephant in the room: cost. Many people assume that making dog food at home is expensive. In reality, it can be pretty economical. Buying ingredients in bulk and utilizing seasonal produce can keep costs down. Plus, the peace of mind that comes from knowing your dogs are eating healthy, balanced meals is priceless.

Then there's the joy of cooking. I find immense pleasure in creating meals for my dogs. It's a labor of love, and the wagging tails and happy barks I get in return make it all worthwhile. It's like baking cookies for your kids, but you're working with chicken and carrots instead of sugar and flour. The principle is the same: nourishing loved ones with wholesome, homemade goodness.

Finally, let's consider the environmental impact. Making dog food at home can significantly reduce packaging waste. Store-bought pet food often comes in plastic bags and aluminum cans, contributing to overflowing landfills. By using fresh ingredients and reusable containers, you're doing right by your dog and our planet.

In summary, the value of homemade dog food is clear: It lets us offer our pets optimal nutrition customized to their specific needs while strengthening the bond we share through cooking. Homemade dog food embodies love, care, and responsibility.

HOW BALANCED NUTRITION BENEFITS YOUR DOG

Giving dogs a well-rounded diet ensures they get the essential nutrients for their health and well-being. Let's delve into the benefits of a balanced diet for dogs and why it's crucial for their long-term vitality.

A balanced diet for dogs includes the right proportions of proteins, fats, carbohydrates, vitamins, and minerals. Each plays a critical role in maintaining optimal health.

Proteins are vital for muscle development, tissue repair, and overall growth. They are composed of amino acids, some of which are essential, meaning dogs must obtain them through their diet. High-quality protein sources such as chicken, beef, fish, and eggs provide these essential amino acids. For instance, once plagued by muscle loss, a neighbor's aging German Shepherd regained significant strength and vitality after switching to a high-protein diet.

Fats are not just a source of energy; they also support cell function, enhance the absorption of fat-soluble vitamins (A, D, E, and K), and contribute to a healthy coat and skin. Omega-3 and Omega-6 fatty acids are particularly beneficial in fish oil and flaxseed. For example, after incorporating these healthy fats into his diet, a friend's French Bulldog with chronic skin issues saw remarkable improvement.

Carbohydrates provide the energy dogs need for their daily activities. While dogs can convert proteins into energy, carbohydrates are a more efficient energy source. Whole grains, vegetables, and fruits are excellent carbohydrate sources that offer fiber, promoting healthy digestion. A local Beagle, once sluggish, became more active after her diet was adjusted to include a balanced amount of carbohydrates.

Vitamins and minerals are crucial for many bodily functions, including bone health, immune support, and neurological function. Fresh vegetables and fruits in a dog's diet ensure they receive a broad spectrum of these vital nutrients. Dogs on balanced diets with adequate vitamins and minerals tend to have more robust immune systems and better overall health, as evidenced by a neighbor's Terrier who rarely falls ill anymore.

Weight Management is another significant benefit of a balanced diet. Dog obesity can cause a range of health problems, such as diabetes, heart disease, and joint issues. Portion control and nutrient-rich, balanced meals help maintain a healthy weight. For instance, my friend's Dachshund, previously struggling with obesity, successfully reached a healthier weight through a carefully managed diet, leading to improved mobility and a better quality of life.

A balanced diet greatly enhances digestive health. Many commercial dog foods contain fillers and artificial additives that can upset a dog's stomach. Fresh, natural ingredients are easier for dogs to digest and can help prevent gastrointestinal issues. A local Labrador with chronic digestive problems experienced significant relief after transitioning to a diet of fresh, whole foods.

A balanced diet also positively impacts behavior and mood. Proper nutrition supports brain health and can lead to improved behavior and a calmer disposition. A neighbor's Border Collie showed reduced anxiety and increased playfulness after my neighbor adjusted the dog's diet to ensure a balance of nutrients.

Longevity and quality of life are the most compelling reasons for providing a balanced diet. Dogs fed a nutrient-rich, balanced diet tend to live longer, healthier lives. The holistic benefits of proper nutrition manifest in better physical health, mental well-being, and a stronger immune system, contributing to an overall higher quality of life.

A balanced diet is fundamental to a dog's health and happiness. It ensures our pets receive the necessary nutrients to thrive, from muscle development and energy production to immune support and digestive health. By investing in their nutrition, we invest in their well-being, fostering healthier, more vibrant lives. This book aims to provide you with the knowledge and tools to create these balanced meals, ensuring your furry friends live their best lives.

TOOLS AND EQUIPMENT

Embarking on making homemade dog food can be both rewarding and a little daunting. But fear not, for with the right tools and equipment, you can transform your kitchen into a haven of healthy, nutritious meals for your furry friends. Here's a guide to the essentials you'll need to get started.

The Basics

First and foremost, let's talk about the basics. Your kitchen likely already has most of what you need, but a few specialized items can make the process smoother and more efficient.

Cutting Boards and Knives: Good sharp knives and a sturdy cutting board are indispensable. Opt for a high-quality chef's knife for chopping meats and vegetables and a smaller paring knife for finer tasks. A dedicated cutting board for dog food preparation can help prevent cross-contamination and keep things hygienic.

Mixing Bowls: Stainless steel or glass mixing bowls in various sizes will serve you well. These are perfect for mixing ingredients, marinating meats, and preparing dough for treats.

Measuring Cups and Spoons: Precision is critical to ensuring your dog gets the right balance of nutrients. Invest in reliable measuring cups and spoons to measure ingredients accurately.

Food Processor or Blender: A food processor or high-speed blender is handy for pureeing vegetables, grinding meats, and mixing ingredients smoothly. This can save you a lot of time, especially when preparing large batches of food.

Saucepans and Stockpots: Depending on your chosen recipes, having a range of saucepans and stockpots will be helpful. These are essential for boiling, simmering, and cooking large quantities of food.

Baking Sheets and Muffin Tins: For baked treats and meals, non-stick baking sheets and muffin tins are a must. Silicone muffin molds are also great for creating portion-sized servings that are easy to store and serve.

Specialized Equipment

Consider adding a few specialized tools to your kitchen arsenal to elevate your homemade dog food preparation.

Slow Cooker or Instant Pot: These appliances are fantastic for making hearty stews and slow-cooked meals that retain their nutritional value. A slow cooker allows you to prepare meals with minimal effort, while an Instant Pot can speed up the cooking process without sacrificing flavor or nutrients.

Dehydrator: A dehydrator is worth the investment if you enjoy making homemade treats. It's perfect for drying fruits, vegetables, and meats into healthy, preservative-free snacks that your dog will love.

Meat Grinder: A meat grinder is invaluable for those who prefer to prepare raw diets or want complete control over the quality of ground meat. It allows you to grind meats and bones to the desired consistency and ensures freshness.

Kitchen Scale: Precision is essential for portion control and ingredient measurements. A digital kitchen scale can help you weigh exact amounts, ensuring your recipes are nutritionally balanced.

Storage Solutions

Preparing homemade dog food often involves making larger batches and storing them for future use. Practical storage solutions are crucial to maintain freshness and prevent spoilage.

Freezer-Safe Containers: Invest in high-quality, BPA-free plastic or glass freezer-safe containers. These are ideal for storing large quantities of dog food. Please ensure they are airtight to prevent freezer burn and preserve the food's nutritional value.

Silicone Freezer Trays: These trays are great for portioning out meals. Once frozen, the portions can be transferred to freezer bags for long-term storage, making it easy to defrost just the right amount of food.

Vacuum Sealer: A vacuum sealer can extend the shelf life of raw and cooked foods by removing air and sealing in freshness. This is especially useful for bulk preparation.

Food Storage Bags: High-quality, resealable food storage bags are convenient for storing treats and portions of food. They take up less space in the freezer, and you can label them with dates and contents for easy organization.

Cleaning and Maintenance

Keeping your tools and equipment clean is vital to prevent contamination and ensure the longevity of your gear.

Dishwasher-Safe Items: Whenever possible, choose dishwasher-safe items to make cleanup easier. High dishwasher temperatures can thoroughly sanitize your tools.

Sanitizing Solutions: To prevent bacterial buildup, regularly sanitize your cutting boards, knives, and work surfaces with a pet-safe sanitizing solution.

Routine Maintenance: Follow the manufacturer's instructions for maintaining appliances like meat grinders and dehydrators. Regular maintenance will ensure they remain in good working condition and last years.

With the right tools and equipment, preparing homemade meals for your dog can be seamless and enjoyable. Armed with these essentials, you'll be ready to create nutritious, delicious dishes that support your pet's health and well-being.

BASIC COOKING TECHNIQUES

Embarking on the journey to prepare homemade meals for your dog is not just a task; it's an act of love and a delightful culinary adventure. The proper cooking techniques can make all the difference in preserving the nutritional value of the ingredients while making the process enjoyable and efficient. Here are some fundamental cooking methods to get you started, infused with warmth, expertise, and friendly guidance, to make your cooking experience for your furry friend a joyous one.

Boiling and Steaming

These are the most straightforward techniques, perfect for preserving the nutrients in meats and vegetables. Boiling is ideal for making broths and softening hard vegetables. Bring a pot of water to a boil, add your ingredients, and cook them until tender.

On the other hand, steaming retains more vitamins and minerals by cooking food gently. A steaming basket or a dedicated steamer will do the trick. This method is excellent for vegetables like carrots, sweet potatoes, leafy greens, fish, and chicken. It's a gentle process that locks in flavors and nutrients.

Baking

Baking is suitable for various dishes, from hearty casseroles to delicious dog biscuits. Preheat your oven to the required temperature, typically around 350°F (175°C), and use a non-stick baking sheet or silicone mold. Baking is perfect for making treats that need to hold their shape, like pumpkin and peanut butter biscuits or meatloaf.

The oven's even heat ensures that food cooks thoroughly, creating a texture that many dogs find irresistible. Plus, the aroma of baking treats will make your kitchen the favorite room in the house.

Slow Cooking

A slow cooker or crockpot can be a lifesaver for busy pet parents. It allows you to prepare large batches of food with minimal effort, and the slow, consistent heat helps retain the ingredients' nutritional value. Add your ingredients to the slow cooker, set it to low, and let it work magic over several hours.

This method is particularly suited for tougher cuts of meat and hearty vegetables that benefit from long, slow cooking times. Think beef stews, chicken casseroles, and lamb with root vegetables. The result is a tender, flavorful meal that your dog will love.

Blending and Pureeing

Blending and pureeing can make meals easier to digest for dogs with dental issues or sensitive stomachs. A high-speed blender or food processor will become your best friend in the kitchen. By blending cooked meats, vegetables, and grains together, you can create smooth, easily digestible meals.

You can also use this technique to incorporate fruits and vegetables that might otherwise be left at the bottom of the bowl. Pureeing spinach, blueberries, or pumpkin with a bit of yogurt can create a nutrient-packed, tasty addition to your dog's diet.

Grilling

Grilling can add a wonderful smoky flavor to your dog's meals, but you should do it carefully. Avoid using seasonings or marinades that contain harmful ingredients like salt, garlic, or onion. Simple grilled meats like chicken breasts or fish can be a delightful treat. Just be sure to cook thoroughly and remove any bones before serving.

Microwaving

While not the most glamorous method, microwaving can quickly and conveniently prepare small amounts of food or reheat leftovers. Use microwave-safe containers and cover the food to retain moisture. Stir well and check the temperature to avoid hot spots that could burn your dog's mouth.

Raw Preparation

Those opting for a raw diet must source high-quality, human-grade meats and follow strict hygiene practices to prevent contamination. Raw feeding involves no cooking, so the focus shifts to handling and storage. Consult with a veterinarian to ensure you safely meet your dog's nutritional needs.

Final Tips

- **Consistency is Fundamental:** Regardless of the method, ensure consistency in your cooking to provide a stable diet for your dog. Sudden changes in texture or preparation can sometimes upset their stomach.
- **Monitor and Adjust:** Pay attention to how your dog responds to different textures and flavors. Some dogs might prefer softer foods, while others might enjoy a bit of crunch.
- **Keep It Simple:** Dogs appreciate simple, wholesome ingredients. There's no need for elaborate seasonings or complex recipes. Focus on fresh, high-quality ingredients and straightforward preparation.

TRANSITIONING YOUR DOG TO HOMEMADE FOOD

Switching your dog to a homemade diet introduces them to a new culinary world, where you craft every meal with love and attention to detail. While rewarding, this transition requires patience and a careful approach to ensure your furry friend adapts smoothly. Here's a guide to making this change as seamless as possible, blending expertise with a touch of warmth and care.

Start Gradually

Dogs, like people, can be creatures of habit, particularly when it comes to their meals. An abrupt change in diet can lead to digestive upset and even reluctance to eat. To avoid this, gradually mix a small amount of homemade food with their regular commercial food. Slowly increase the proportion of homemade food over two weeks while decreasing the commercial food. This gradual shift helps your dog's digestive system adjust to the new diet without stress.

Here is the 14-day dog's transition plan to home-cooked meals in a chart form:

Days	Day	Morning	Evening	Instructions
Days 1-3	1	75% old food, 25% new home-cooked meal	Same as morning	Mix the new food thoroughly with the old food. Monitor for any immediate adverse reactions.
	2	75% old food, 25% new home-cooked meal	Same as morning	Continue mixing and observing your dog's reaction. Look for any signs of digestive upset.
	3	75% old food, 25% new home-cooked meal	Same as morning	Maintain the same ratio. Monitor stool consistency and energy levels.
Days 4-6	4	50% old food, 50% new home-cooked meal	Same as morning	Gradually increase the proportion of new food. Mix well and observe for any changes in behavior or digestion.
	5	50% old food, 50% new home-cooked meal	Same as morning	Maintain the ratio and continue to monitor. Take note of your dog's stool quality and energy levels.
	6	50% old food, 50% new home-cooked meal	Same as morning	Continue with the 50/50 ratio. Ensure your dog is adjusting well to the increasing amount of new food.
Days 7-9	7	25% old food, 75% new home-cooked meal	Same as morning	Increase the amount of new food to three-quarters of the meal. Monitor for any digestive issues.
	8	25% old food, 75% new home-cooked meal	Same as morning	Maintain the ratio. Keep a close watch on your dog's health and energy.
	9	25% old food, 75% new home-cooked meal	Same as morning	Continue with the same proportions. Ensure your dog is responding well to the new diet.
Days 10-12	10	10% old food, 90% new home-cooked	Same as morning	Further decrease the old food to just a small portion. Observe your dog closely

Days	Day	Morning	Evening	Instructions
		meal		for any signs of intolerance.
	11	10% old food, 90% new home-cooked meal	Same as morning	Maintain the 90/10 ratio. Check for consistent energy levels and stool quality.
	12	10% old food, 90% new home-cooked meal	Same as morning	Continue with the same ratio. Ensure your dog's digestive system is adapting well.
Days 13-14	13	100% new home-cooked meal	Same as morning	Finally, serve only the new home-cooked meals. Monitor for any last-minute issues.
	14	100% new home-cooked meal	Same as morning	Your dog should now be fully transitioned to home-cooked meals. Continue to monitor their health and make any necessary adjustments.

Monitor Your Dog's Response

Transitioning your dog to a new diet is a process that requires careful attention and observation. Each dog is unique, and their response to dietary changes can vary significantly. Here are some detailed steps and considerations to ensure a smooth transition and maintain your dog's health and well-being:

1. Observing your dog's digestive health is crucial, especially during diet transitions. Signs of digestive discomfort include vomiting, which can occasionally happen but becomes a concern if frequent. Diarrhea, characterized by loose stools, is common initially, but persistent diarrhea may indicate an intolerance or allergy. Constipation, marked by difficulty passing stools or straining, can also signal that the new diet does not agree with your dog. It is essential to monitor the frequency and consistency of your dog's stools; ideally, they should be regular and well-formed. Please make sure to note and address any significant changes promptly.

2. Monitoring your dog's energy levels is essential to ensure their health. A healthy dog should display consistent energy levels suitable for their age and breed. Decreased activity, lethargy, or excessive sleeping might indicate an issue with their new diet. Additionally, observe your dog's performance during walks or playtime. Reduced stamina or reluctance to engage in physical activity could suggest that the new food needs to provide more nutrition.

3. Assessing your dog's coat and skin condition is essential for gauging their health. A shiny, soft coat indicates good health, so be attentive to any signs of dullness, excessive shedding, or bald spots. Additionally, check your dog's skin for dryness, flakiness, or irritation. Persistent scratching or the appearance of hot spots may indicate food allergies or sensitivities.

4. Behavioral changes in your dog can offer valuable insights into their well-being. Take any signs of depression, anxiety, or irritability seriously. A happy, content dog will generally be more playful and affectionate. Additionally, pay attention to your dog's eating habits.

Reluctance to eat the new food or appearing overly hungry can indicate digestive discomfort or a dislike for the new diet.

If your dog shows signs of distress, slow down the transition process. Mix smaller amounts of the new food with the old food to allow their system more time to adjust.

Introduce a Variety of Foods

One of the joys of homemade dog food is the variety of ingredients you can offer. However, it's essential to introduce new foods slowly and one at a time. This approach allows you to identify any food sensitivities or allergies. Start with familiar proteins like chicken or beef, and gradually add vegetables, grains, and healthy fats. This variety ensures a balanced diet and keeps your dog excited about mealtime.

Maintain Nutritional Balance

As you transition to homemade food, it's crucial to maintain a balanced diet. Dogs require specific ratios of proteins, fats, carbohydrates, vitamins, and minerals. Here's a general guideline for nutrient distribution:

- Proteins: 25-30%
- Fats: 10-15%
- Carbohydrates: 55-65%.

Remember, you're not alone in this journey. Consult with your veterinarian or a canine nutritionist to ensure the recipes you use meet your dog's nutritional needs. Their expertise and guidance will help you navigate this transition with confidence. Supplements, such as calcium for bone health or omega-3 fatty acids for skin and coat health, might be necessary to fill any gaps.

Portion Control

Switching to homemade food can be easy, overfeeding or underfeeding, especially as portion sizes can be less intuitive than scooping out kibble. Use a kitchen scale to measure precise portions based on your dog's weight, age, and activity level. Maintaining proper portion control helps achieve a healthy weight and prevents nutritional imbalances. Please see the chapter **Portion Sizing and Weight Control** for more details further.

Consistency and Routine

Dogs thrive on routine, so try to keep mealtime schedules consistent. Feeding them simultaneously each day provides stability and helps regulate their digestive system. Additionally, serving meals in a quiet, distraction-free environment can help make the transition smoother and more enjoyable for your dog.

Stay Patient and Positive

Remember, Rome wasn't built in a day, and neither is a successful transition to homemade food. Patience is crucial. Some dogs may take to the new diet quickly, while others might be more hesitant. Stay positive and encouraging, offering praise and treats to reinforce good behavior. If your dog is particularly resistant, try warming the food slightly or adding a bit of low-sodium broth to enhance its aroma and appeal.

Document the Journey

Keep a journal to document your dog's transition to homemade food. Note any changes in their health and preferences. Keep a daily log of your dog's stool consistency, energy levels, coat condition, and overall behavior. This detailed record will be invaluable for adjusting the diet and consultations with your veterinarian. It also serves as a testament to your care and attention to your dog's well-being.

Consult the Experts

Throughout this process, maintain an open line of communication with your veterinarian. Regular check-ups and discussions about your dog's diet can help ensure they're receiving the best possible care. A professional's guidance can make the transition smoother and address any concerns.

Celebrate the Milestones

Transitioning to homemade food is a significant step towards enhancing your dog's health and happiness. Celebrate the milestones, whether it's the first successful meal or noticeable improvements in their coat and energy levels. These moments of progress are a testament to your dedication and love for your furry friend.

SAFETY TIPS AND STORAGE GUIDELINES

Your role in ensuring the safety and proper storage of homemade dog food is crucial. By following these guidelines, you are taking a proactive step toward keeping your furry friend healthy and happy. Here's how to navigate the landscape of food safety and storage with ease and confidence, knowing that you are making a difference in your dog's well-being.

Prioritize Hygiene

Maintaining impeccable hygiene is the bedrock of safe food preparation. Always start by washing your hands thoroughly before and after handling any ingredients. This simple step helps prevent the spread of bacteria and keeps you and your dog safe.

Clean Equipment

Ensure that all utensils, cutting boards, and bowls used in preparing your dog's food are clean. Hot, soapy water is your best friend here. Consider using separate tools for dog food preparation to avoid cross-contamination with your own meals.

Handle Raw Meat with Care

Raw meat can harbor bacteria like Salmonella and E. coli, harming you and your dog. Always keep raw meat separate from other ingredients and clean any surfaces and utensils that come into contact immediately. If you feed raw, consult your veterinarian for best practices and source high-quality, safe-to-eat meats.

Cook Meats to Safe Temperatures

Cooking meat to safe temperatures is critical to ensuring the health and safety of your dog's meals. Meat can harbor harmful pathogens, including bacteria such as Salmonella, E. coli, and Listeria, as well as parasites like Toxoplasma and Trichinella. These pathogens can lead to foodborne illnesses, which can be severe and even fatal for dogs. Cooking meat to the appropriate temperatures kills these pathogens, ensuring the food is safe for consumption.

Ensure you cook different types of meat at the appropriate temperatures to destroy all harmful organisms. Here are the recommended safe cooking temperatures for common meats used in homemade dog food:

- Cook chicken and turkey to an internal temperature of 165°F (74°C) to eradicate any bacteria, particularly Salmonella and Campylobacter.
- Cook ground beef and lamb to an internal temperature of 160°F (71°C). Whole cuts like steaks or roasts should reach at least 145°F (63°C) and be allowed to rest for at least three minutes before serving.
- Cook pork to an internal temperature of 160°F (71°C) to eliminate Trichinella spiralis, a parasite that causes trichinosis.
- Cook fish to an internal temperature of 145°F (63°C) to eliminate parasites and harmful bacteria.

Practical Tips for Ensuring Safe Cooking Temperatures:

1. **Use a Meat Thermometer:** The most reliable way to ensure meat has reached a safe temperature is by using a meat thermometer. Insert the thermometer into the thickest part of the meat, avoiding bone and fat, for an accurate reading.

2. **Allow for Resting Time:** For whole cuts of meat like steaks and roasts, allowing the meat to rest for a few minutes after cooking helps stabilize the temperature and kills any residual bacteria.

3. **Avoid Cross-Contamination:** When preparing raw meat, use separate cutting boards, utensils, and surfaces to avoid cross-contamination with other foods. After handling raw meat, wash your hands, utensils, and surfaces with hot, soapy water.

4. **Store Meat Properly:** Store raw meat at a safe temperature (below 40°F or 4°C) and cook it within a few days of purchase. Freeze any meat that you will not use immediately.

5. **Cook in Batches:** If you're preparing large quantities of food, cook the meat in batches to ensure even cooking and avoid overcrowding the pan or oven, which can lead to uneven cooking and unsafe temperatures.

6. **Check Visual Cues:** While temperature is the most reliable indicator, visual cues can help. Cooked poultry should have clear juices with no pink meat, beef, and pork should be brown or grey inside, and fish should be opaque and flake easily with a fork.

Choose Safe Ingredients

Not all human foods are safe for dogs. Familiarize yourself with ingredients that are toxic to dogs. Double-check before introducing any new ingredient into your dog's diet to ensure it's safe. Please see the chapter **Foods to Avoid** for more details further.

Store Fresh Food Properly

Once you've prepared your dog's meals, proper storage is critical to maintaining freshness and safety. Store fresh food in airtight containers to prevent spoilage and contamination. Refrigerate meals you consume within a few days, and freeze the rest to extend their shelf life.

Freezing Guidelines

Freezing homemade dog food is an excellent way to preserve its nutritional value and ensure you always have meals ready. Store food in BPA-free plastic containers, silicone trays, or freezer-safe glass jars. Label each container with the contents and date of preparation to keep track of freshness. This simple step clarifies how long food has been stored and ensures you use the oldest stock first, maintaining a rotation that keeps the food fresh. You can typically store frozen dog food for up to three months.

Defrost Safely

When it's time to use the frozen food, defrost it in the refrigerator rather than at room temperature to prevent bacterial growth. This process might take a little longer, but it is the safest method. If you're in a hurry, you can defrost food in the microwave, but be sure to stir it well and check for hot spots that could burn your dog's mouth.

The Importance of Proper Portioning

Proper portioning ensures your dog gets the right amount of food and helps with storage. Divide meals into single-serving portions before freezing. This makes it easy to defrost only what you need, reducing waste and maintaining food quality. Please see the chapter **Portion Sizing and Weight Control** to calculate portion sizes.

Check for Spoilage

Regularly check the food you store for any signs of spoilage, such as changes in color, texture, or smell. If you're ever in doubt about the freshness of the food, it's better to err on the side of caution and discard it.

Invest in Quality Storage Containers

High-quality storage containers that are easy to clean and seal tightly are essential. Glass containers with airtight lids are an excellent choice as they do not retain odors and are safe for the refrigerator and freezer. Silicone freezer trays are also handy for portioning meals and are easy to pop food out of when needed.

Avoid Overloading the Freezer

Do not overload your freezer with too much dog food at a time. Ensure enough space for air to circulate the containers to keep them at a consistent temperature. This helps prevent partial thawing and refreezing, which can compromise the quality and safety of the food.

UNDERSTANDING MACRONUTRIENTS: PROTEINS, CARBS, AND FATS

Understanding the fundamentals of nutrition is paramount when nourishing our canine companions. At the heart of this lies the trio of macronutrients: proteins, carbohydrates, and fats. Each plays a vital role in maintaining your dog's health, energy, and overall well-being. Let's delve into these essential components with the warmth and expertise you'd expect from a devoted pet parent and home cook.

Proteins: The Building Blocks of Life

Proteins are more than just a dietary component; they are the foundation of your dog's diet, involved in every biological process from muscle development to immune function. Dogs, like humans, cannot produce all the amino acids they need internally. Our pets must obtain these essential amino acids through their diet. The primary amino acids that dogs require include:

- Arginine
- Histidine
- Isoleucine
- Leucine
- Lysine
- Methionine
- Phenylalanine
- Threonine
- Tryptophan
- Valine

Lean meats like chicken, beef, turkey, and fish are high-quality protein sources. These provide the essential amino acids that support growth, tissue repair, and metabolic functions. Eggs and dairy products such as yogurt and cottage cheese are also excellent protein sources. Plant-based proteins, such as lentils and chickpeas, can complement these sources, though they should not be the primary protein due to lower amino acid availability.

Carbohydrates: The Energy Providers

Carbohydrates often get a mixed reception in the human diet world, but for dogs, they are a vital energy source. They fuel your dog's daily activities and help maintain a steady blood sugar level.

Whole grains like brown rice, oats, and barley and vegetables like sweet potatoes and carrots are excellent carbohydrate sources. These also offer dietary fiber, which aids in digestion and keeps the gastrointestinal tract healthy. Fiber can be soluble or insoluble, and each serving has different functions. Soluble fiber in oats and legumes helps regulate blood sugar and lower cholesterol levels. Insoluble fiber in whole grains and vegetables adds bulk to the stool and aids in regular bowel movements.

Fats: The Energy-Dense Nutrients

Fats are often misunderstood but are crucial for your dog's health. They provide a concentrated source of energy, support cell function, and aid in absorbing fat-soluble vitamins (A, D, E, and K).

Essential fatty acids, such as Omega-3 and Omega-6, play vital roles in maintaining healthy skin and a shiny coat, reducing inflammation, and supporting brain health.

Good sources of healthy fats include fish oil, flaxseed oil, and animal fats from meats.

Balancing the Trio

Achieving the right balance of proteins, carbohydrates, and fats is the key to a well-rounded diet. Each macronutrient serves a unique purpose, creating a synergistic effect that promotes overall health. Please consult your veterinarian to determine the ideal macronutrient ratios for your dog based on age, breed, activity level, and any specific health needs.

For puppies, the focus might be on higher protein and fat to support rapid growth and development. On the other hand, senior dogs benefit from a diet lower in fat and higher in easily digestible proteins and fiber to support a slower metabolism and prevent weight gain.

VITAL VITAMINS AND MINERALS

Navigating the world of homemade dog food involves more than just picking out proteins, carbs, and fats. To nourish our furry friends, we must dive into vitamins and minerals, the unsung heroes of a balanced diet. Though required in smaller amounts, these micronutrients are crucial in maintaining your dog's health and vitality. Let's explore the essential vitamins and minerals, ensuring your homemade meals are delicious and nutritionally complete.

Vitamins: The Tiny Titans

Vitamin A

Vitamin A is indispensable for vision, immune function, and cell growth. Liver, fish oils, and orange vegetables like carrots and sweet potatoes contain it in abundance. This fat-soluble vitamin helps maintain healthy skin and coat, supports night vision, and boosts the immune system. Think of it as the guardian of your dog's outer defenses and sharp eyesight.

B Vitamins

The B vitamin family, including B1 (thiamine), B2 (riboflavin), B6 (pyridoxine), and B12 (cobalamin), supports energy metabolism, nervous system function, and red blood cell formation. These vitamins are abundant in meats, eggs, and dairy products. They act like the spark plugs in your dog's body, keeping everything running smoothly and efficiently.

Vitamin C

While dogs can synthesize Vitamin C independently, additional sources from fruits and vegetables like blueberries and bell peppers can be beneficial. Vitamin C is an antioxidant that protects cells from damage and supports collagen production, which is vital for joint health and wound healing.

Vitamin D

Vitamin D is crucial for calcium absorption and bone health. Sunlight exposure and dietary sources like fish and eggs provide it. This vitamin is the gatekeeper that ensures calcium, and phosphorus do their jobs in building and maintaining strong bones and teeth.

Vitamin E

Vitamin E is a potent antioxidant found in vegetable oils, nuts, and leafy greens. It supports skin health, immune function, and cellular repair. Consider it the body's natural defense against oxidative damage, keeping cells healthy and vibrant.

Vitamin K

Leafy greens and the liver provide Vitamin K, essential for blood clotting and bone health. This vitamin acts like a regulator, ensuring that your dog's blood coagulates properly and their bones remain strong and resilient.

Minerals: The Building Blocks

Calcium and Phosphorus

Calcium and phosphorus are vital for bone and teeth formation, muscle function, and nerve transmission. Dairy products, bones, and fish contain these minerals, which work together. They form the structural foundation of your dog's body, supporting growth and maintenance.

Potassium

Potassium supports nerve function, muscle contractions, and fluid balance. Bananas, sweet potatoes, and spinach contain it. This mineral acts like an electrolyte, maintaining proper hydration and nerve impulses.

Sodium and Chloride

Sodium and chloride, which are present in meat, fish, and eggs, help maintain fluid balance. These minerals are crucial for maintaining cellular homeostasis and ensuring proper muscle and nerve function.

Magnesium

Magnesium plays a role in over 300 biochemical reactions in the body, including energy production and muscle function. Leafy greens, nuts, and seeds contain it. Think of magnesium as the behind-the-scenes worker that keeps the body's processes humming smoothly.

Iron

Red meat, liver, and leafy greens contain iron necessary for oxygen transport in the blood. This mineral is the lifeline for every cell, ensuring it receives the oxygen needed for energy production and overall vitality.

Zinc

Zinc supports immune function, skin health, and wound healing. It is present in meat, fish, and eggs. Consider zinc the body's repairman, fixing damaged cells and supporting immune responses.

Copper

Copper aids in the formation of red blood cells and connective tissue. Liver, seafood, and whole grains contain it. This mineral ensures that your dog's body can properly utilize iron and maintain healthy connective tissues.

Balancing Act

Ensuring your dog receives the right balance of vitamins and minerals is crucial. Over-supplementation can be as harmful as deficiencies. Consult your veterinarian to determine your dog's needs based on age, breed, and health status. This professional guidance helps tailor the diet to your dog's unique requirements, ensuring optimal nutrition without any guesswork.

Sourcing and Supplementing

While whole foods are the best sources of vitamins and minerals, sometimes supplementation is necessary to fill any gaps. High-quality supplements can provide additional support, especially for dogs with specific health concerns or dietary restrictions. Always choose supplements designed specifically for dogs and consult your vet before adding them to your dog's diet.

COMMON FOODS AND THEIR NUTRITIONAL BENEFITS

The pantry can be a treasure trove of nutritional gems for feeding our dogs. Many common foods we use in our kitchens offer a wealth of benefits for our canine companions, contributing to their overall health and well-being. Here's a guide to some everyday ingredients and the nutritional perks they bring to the table for your furry friends.

Lean Meats

Chicken, Beef, Turkey, and Fish: These proteins are the bedrock of your dog's diet, essential for muscle development, tissue repair, and energy. Chicken and turkey are lean and easy to digest, while beef offers rich iron and zinc content, critical for maintaining energy and immune function. Fish, particularly salmon, is a stellar source of omega-3 fatty acids, which promote a shiny coat and reduce inflammation.

Eggs

Eggs are a nearly perfect food packed with high-quality protein, essential vitamins, and minerals. They provide all the essential amino acids your dog needs, vitamins A, D, and E, and minerals like selenium and riboflavin. A scrambled egg added to your dog's meal can boost their protein intake and add a bit of variety.

Offal

Liver, Kidneys, and Heart: Offal, or organ meats, are incredibly nutrient-dense and should be a regular part of your dog's diet. The liver packs in vitamins A, B, iron, and folate. Kidneys provide high levels of vitamins A, B12, riboflavin, iron, and zinc. The heart is rich in taurine, an essential amino acid that supports heart health. These organs provide a powerful nutritional punch, supporting overall vitality and wellness.

Vegetables

Carrots: These vibrant roots contain beta-carotene, which the body converts to vitamin A. This vitamin is crucial for maintaining good vision, a robust immune system, and healthy skin and coat.

Sweet Potatoes and Pumpkins are excellent dietary fiber sources, aiding digestion and providing a steady release of energy. They also contain vitamins A and C, which support immune health and skin integrity.

Leafy Greens

Spinach, Kale, and Broccoli: Dark leafy greens are nutritional powerhouses. Spinach and kale are rich in iron, calcium, and vitamins A, C, and K, supporting bone health, immune function, and overall vitality. Broccoli offers a substantial amount of fiber and vitamin C, aiding digestion and boosting the immune system.

Fruits

Blueberries: These tiny berries are antioxidant giants. They help combat oxidative stress, which can damage cells, and support brain health. They're also a good source of fiber, vitamin C, and vitamin K.

Apples: Apples are a great source of vitamins A and C and fiber. Just remove the seeds and core, as they can be harmful. Apples can help keep your dog's teeth clean and freshen their breath.

Bananas: These tropical favorites provide potassium essential for heart and muscle function. They're also rich in vitamins B6 and C and fiber, making them a wholesome snack or meal addition.

Whole Grains

Brown Rice, Oats, and Quinoa: Whole grains are excellent sources of carbohydrates, providing the energy your dog needs to stay active. Brown rice is gentle on the digestive system and supports bowel health. Oats pack vitamins B and E and essential minerals like zinc and iron. Although technically a seed, quinoa is treated as a grain and offers a complete protein profile, making it a valuable addition for dogs with gluten sensitivities.

Healthy Fats

Fish Oil, Flaxseed Oil, and Coconut Oil: These fats are vital for energy, brain function, and maintaining a healthy coat and skin. Fish oil is rich in omega-3 fatty acids, which reduce inflammation and support cardiovascular health. Flaxseed oil is another excellent source of omega-3s, particularly for dogs with fish allergies. Coconut oil provides medium-chain triglycerides (MCTs), which can boost energy levels and improve cognitive function.

Herbs and Spices

Parsley: This herb freshens breath and provides vitamins C and K. It has anti-inflammatory properties and can aid digestion.

Turmeric: Known for its anti-inflammatory and antioxidant properties, turmeric can support joint health and overall wellness. Adding a small amount to your dog's food can provide these benefits without overwhelming their palate.

Ginger: This root is excellent for aiding digestion and soothing an upset stomach. It also has anti-inflammatory properties, which can benefit older dogs with arthritis.

Yogurt and Cottage Cheese

These dairy products are rich in protein and calcium, supporting strong bones and teeth. They also contain probiotics, which promote a healthy gut microbiome. Opt for plain, unsweetened versions to avoid added sugars and artificial sweeteners.

Nuts and Seeds

Pumpkin Seeds: These tiny seeds contain nutrients, including magnesium, manganese, iron, zinc, and protein. They also contain antioxidants and essential fatty acids.

Chia Seeds: These tiny seeds are a powerhouse of nutrition, offering omega-3 fatty acids, fiber, and protein. They can help with digestion, energy levels, and overall health.

FOODS TO AVOID

While the world of homemade dog food offers a rich tapestry of nourishing options, it also harbors potential hazards that can turn a well-intentioned meal into a dangerous one. Navigating this culinary minefield requires a keen understanding of foods that, while harmless or beneficial to us, can pose significant risks to our canine companions. Let's explore some common culprits, ensuring our beloved dogs stay safe and healthy.

Chocolate

A beloved treat for humans, chocolate is a severe no-no for dogs. It contains theobromine and caffeine, both of which are toxic to dogs. Even small amounts can cause vomiting, diarrhea, and excessive thirst, while larger doses can lead to abnormal heart rhythms, seizures, and potentially fatal outcomes. Dark chocolate and unsweetened baking chocolate are hazardous due to their higher theobromine content.

Grapes and Raisins

These seemingly innocent fruits can cause acute kidney failure in dogs. The toxic substance within grapes and raisins remains unidentified, but even small quantities can lead to severe reactions. Symptoms include vomiting, lethargy, and loss of appetite, often progressing to more severe complications. Keep these out of reach at all costs.

Onions and Garlic

Both onions and garlic, whether raw, cooked, or powdered, contain compounds that can damage your dog's red blood cells, leading to anemia. While garlic in small doses might have some health benefits, the risks generally outweigh the advantages, and it's best to avoid it altogether. Symptoms of toxicity include weakness, vomiting, and breathlessness.

Avocado

Avocados contain persin, a fungicidal toxin that can cause vomiting and diarrhea in dogs. While the fleshy part of the fruit is less toxic, the pit, skin, and leaves contain higher levels of persin and pose a choking hazard. It's best to steer clear of this creamy fruit when preparing your dog's meals.

Xylitol

This artificial sweetener in many sugar-free products like gum, candy, and baked goods is highly toxic to dogs. Even a tiny amount can cause a rapid release of insulin, leading to hypoglycemia (low blood sugar), seizures, liver failure, and even death. Always check labels carefully and avoid anything that contains xylitol.

Alcohol

Alcoholic beverages and foods containing alcohol can cause serious health issues for dogs, including vomiting, diarrhea, difficulty breathing, and even death. Dogs are far more sensitive to alcohol than humans, and it's essential to ensure they never have access to it.

Macadamia Nuts

These nuts contain an unknown toxin that can cause weakness, vomiting, tremors, and hyperthermia in dogs. Even small amounts can lead to severe symptoms, so it's best to avoid them entirely.

Caffeine

Caffeine, found in coffee, tea, energy drinks, and certain medications, can be harmful to dogs. It stimulates the nervous system, leading to restlessness, rapid breathing, heart palpitations, and muscle tremors. Ensure your dog has no access to caffeinated substances.

Raw Dough

Raw dough, particularly yeast dough, poses two significant risks to dogs. Firstly, as the dough rises in their stomach, it can cause bloating and potentially life-threatening torsion. Secondly, the fermentation process produces alcohol, which can lead to alcohol poisoning. Always keep raw dough out of reach.

Raw Eggs and Fish

While raw diets can be beneficial, certain raw foods carry risks. Raw eggs can contain Salmonella or E. coli, leading to food poisoning. Additionally, an enzyme in raw egg whites can interfere with the absorption of biotin, a B vitamin, causing skin and coat problems. Raw fish, particularly salmon, can contain parasites that are harmful to dogs. To feed raw, you must source these foods carefully and consult your veterinarian.

High-Sodium Foods

Foods with high sodium content, such as processed meats, chips, and pretzels, can lead to excessive thirst and urination and, in severe cases, sodium ion poisoning. Symptoms include vomiting, diarrhea, tremors, and seizures. Keep salty snacks and processed foods away from your dog's diet.

Bones

Cooked bones, especially poultry bones, can splinter and cause choking or severe injuries to your dog's digestive tract. Even raw bones, while generally safer, should be given under supervision to prevent choking and ensure they're appropriate for your dog's size and chewing habits.

Fat Trimmings and Greasy Foods

Excessive fat can cause pancreatitis in dogs, a painful and potentially life-threatening condition. Avoid feeding your dog fatty cuts of meat or greasy leftovers, and instead opt for lean protein sources.

Dairy Products

While not toxic, many dogs are lactose intolerant and can experience digestive upset, including diarrhea and gas, after consuming dairy products. If you choose to include dairy in your dog's diet, do so sparingly and observe how they react.

Keeping our dogs safe and healthy involves more than providing nutritious food; it also means being vigilant about potential dangers. Understanding and avoiding these hazardous foods ensures your meal is delicious and safe.

PORTION SIZING AND WEIGHT CONTROL

Crafting the perfect diet for your dog is like tailoring a bespoke suit — every measurement matters and attention to detail ensures the best fit.

Proper portion control is crucial for your dog's health and well-being, as it ensures they receive all necessary nutrients without overindulging. Here's a step-by-step guide to calculating the daily portion size of dog food based on weight, activity level, and nutrient content.

Step 1: Determine Your Dog's Ideal Weight

The first step in portion control is identifying your dog's ideal weight. This is crucial because you should base feeding recommendations on your dog's optimal weight, not their current weight if they are overweight or underweight.

Below is a table listing the ideal weight ranges for the 50 popular dog breeds in the USA:

Breed	Ideal Weight Range (lbs / kg)
Labrador Retriever	55 - 80 lbs / 25 - 36 kg
French Bulldog	16 - 28 lbs / 7 - 13 kg
German Shepherd	50 - 90 lbs / 23 - 41 kg
Golden Retriever	55 - 75 lbs / 25 - 34 kg
Bulldog	40 - 50 lbs / 18 - 23 kg
Poodle (Standard)	45 - 70 lbs / 20 - 32 kg
Beagle	20 - 25 lbs / 9 - 11 kg
Rottweiler	80 - 135 lbs / 36 - 61 kg
German Shorthaired Pointer	45 - 70 lbs / 20 - 32 kg
Dachshund	16 - 32 lbs / 7 - 14 kg
Pembroke Welsh Corgi	25 - 30 lbs / 11 - 14 kg
Australian Shepherd	40 - 65 lbs / 18 - 29 kg
Yorkshire Terrier	4 - 7 lbs / 1.8 - 3.2 kg
Boxer	55 - 70 lbs / 25 - 32 kg
Great Dane	110 - 175 lbs / 50 - 79 kg
Siberian Husky	35 - 60 lbs / 16 - 27 kg
Cavalier King Charles Spaniel	13 - 18 lbs / 6 - 8 kg
Doberman Pinscher	60 - 100 lbs / 27 - 45 kg
Miniature Schnauzer	11 - 20 lbs / 5 - 9 kg
Shih Tzu	9 - 16 lbs / 4 - 7 kg
Boston Terrier	10 - 25 lbs / 4.5 - 11 kg
Pomeranian	3 - 7 lbs / 1.4 - 3.2 kg
Havanese	7 - 13 lbs / 3 - 6 kg
Shetland Sheepdog	15 - 25 lbs / 7 - 11 kg
Brittany	30 - 40 lbs / 14 - 18 kg
Bernese Mountain Dog	70 - 115 lbs / 32 - 52 kg
Pug	14 - 18 lbs / 6 - 8 kg
English Springer Spaniel	40 - 50 lbs / 18 - 23 kg
Mastiff	120 - 230 lbs / 54 - 104 kg
Cocker Spaniel	20 - 30 lbs / 9 - 14 kg
Vizsla	45 - 65 lbs / 20 - 29 kg
Cane Corso	90 - 120 lbs / 41 - 54 kg

Breed	Ideal Weight Range (lbs / kg)
Chihuahua	3 - 6 lbs / 1.4 - 2.7 kg
Border Collie	30 - 45 lbs / 14 - 20 kg
Basset Hound	40 - 65 lbs / 18 - 29 kg
Weimaraner	55 - 90 lbs / 25 - 41 kg
Belgian Malinois	40 - 80 lbs / 18 - 36 kg
Newfoundland	100 - 150 lbs / 45 - 68 kg
Collie	50 - 75 lbs / 23 - 34 kg
Bichon Frise	12 - 18 lbs / 5 - 8 kg
Rhodesian Ridgeback	70 - 85 lbs / 32 - 39 kg
West Highland White Terrier	15 - 20 lbs / 7 - 9 kg
Shiba Inu	17 - 23 lbs / 8 - 10 kg
Chesapeake Bay Retriever	55 - 80 lbs / 25 - 36 kg
Akita	70 - 130 lbs / 32 - 59 kg
St. Bernard	120 - 180 lbs / 54 - 82 kg
Bloodhound	80 - 110 lbs / 36 - 50 kg
Bullmastiff	100 - 130 lbs / 45 - 59 kg
Australian Cattle Dog	35 - 50 lbs / 16 - 23 kg
Soft Coated Wheaten Terrier	30 - 40 lbs / 14 - 18 kg

Individual dogs may vary from the ideal weight range within a breed due to age, sex, and overall health. For mixed-breed dogs, consider the dominant breed traits or consult a veterinarian for the most accurate assessment of ideal weight. Always seek personalized advice from a veterinarian, especially if your dog's weight falls outside of these ranges or if you have concerns about their health.

Step 2: Assess Activity Levels
Dogs' caloric needs vary significantly with their activity levels. Classify your dog into one of the following categories:

- **Inactive/Senior:** These dogs require fewer calories due to lower energy expenditure.
- **Moderately Active:** Dogs that engage in regular, moderate exercise.
- **Active/Working:** High-energy dogs that participate in rigorous physical activity.
- **Puppies/Growing Dogs:** These dogs have higher energy requirements than adult dogs because they need additional calories to support their development.

Step 3: Calculate Daily Caloric Needs
Estimate your dog's daily caloric needs using the Resting Energy Requirement (RER) formula (you can use any free exponent calculator online):

$$\text{RER} = 70 \times (\text{Ideal Weight in kg})^{0.75}$$

Then, adjust the RER based on activity level using these multipliers:
- **Inactive/Senior:** RER $\times$ 1.2
- **Moderately Active:** RER $\times$ 1.6
- **Active/Working:** RER $\times$ 2.0

- **Puppies/Growing Dogs:** RER $\times$ 3.0 (0-3 months), RER $\times$ 2.5 (3-6 months), RER $\times$ 2.0 (6-12 months for small and medium breeds/18-24 months for larger breeds)

Step 4: Calculate Daily Portion Size

Determine the caloric content of your homemade dog food per gram. Calculate the correct daily portion size using the formula:

$$\text{Daily Portion (grams)} = \frac{Daily\ Caloric\ Needs}{Calories\ per\ Gram\ of\ Food}$$

Example Calculation

Let's walk through an example of a moderately active, 10 kg French Bulldog:
1. Ideal Weight: 10 kg
2. Activity Level: Moderately Active
3. RER Calculation:

$$\text{RER} = 70 \times (10 \text{ kg})^{0.75}$$
$$\text{RER} = 70 \times 5.62$$
$$\text{RER} \approx 393.4 \text{ kcal/day}$$

Adjusted Caloric Needs:

$$393.4 \times 1.6 = 629.44 \text{ kcal/day}$$

4. Then let's take, for example, the recipe for Chicken and Vegetable Casserole. It has 0.67 kcal/g.

$$\text{Daily Portion} = \frac{629.44\ kcal/day}{0.67\ kcal/g} \approx 939.46 \text{ grams}$$

So, a moderately active, 10 kg French Bulldog requires 939.46 g (33.13 oz) of Chicken and Vegetable Casserole per day. This portion size ensures the dog's caloric needs are met according to their activity level.

Step 5: Monitor and Adjust

Regularly monitor your dog's weight and body condition. Adjust portions as necessary to maintain a healthy weight. Use the following **Body Condition Score (BCS) Chart** to evaluate your dog's physical condition:

BCS Score	Description	Visual Indicators	Touch Indicators
1	Emaciated	Ribs, spine, and hip bones are visible from a distance. Waist and abdominal tuck are very pronounced.	No noticeable body fat or significant muscle loss.
2	Very Thin	Ribs, spine, and hip bones are easily visible. Waist and abdominal tuck are prominent.	Minimal body fat, noticeable muscle loss.
3	Thin	Ribs, spine, and hip bones are visible. Waist and abdominal tuck are visible.	Some body fat is present, but not enough to cover bones. Slight muscle loss.
4	Underweight	Ribs can be easily felt but are not prominent. Waist and abdominal tuck are present.	There is a slight fat cover over the ribs and spine. Minimal muscle loss.
5	Ideal	Ribs can be felt without excess fat cover. The waist is visible when viewed from above. Abdominal tuck is present.	No excessive fat deposits. Well-proportioned body.
6	Overweight	Ribs are difficult to feel under a moderate fat cover. The waist is not easily visible. The abdominal tuck is less pronounced.	Slight fat deposits over the back and base of the tail.
7	Heavy	Ribs are hard to feel under a heavy fat cover. The waist is barely visible or absent. No abdominal tuck.	Noticeable fat deposits over the back, base of the tail, and chest.
8	Obese	Ribs are tough to feel under a thick fat cover. No visible waist. Abdominal sag is present.	Heavy fat deposits over the back, base of the tail, and chest. Significant fat deposits around the neck and limbs.
9	Severely Obese	Ribs cannot be felt under a very thick fat cover. No waist. Marked abdominal sag.	Extensive fat deposits over the entire body. Severe fat deposits around the neck, limbs, and base of the tail.

How to Use the BCS Chart

1. Visual Assessment. Look at your dog from above and from the side. Compare their body shape to the descriptions in the chart.

2. Hands-On Assessment. Feel your dog's ribs, spine, and hip bones. Compare what you feel with the descriptions in the chart.

3. Recording Scores. Regularly assess and record your dog's BCS to track any changes. This helps in adjusting portion sizes and diet as needed.

4. Consulting a Veterinarian. If your dog's BCS is significantly below or above the ideal range (4-6), consult your veterinarian for advice on dietary adjustments and health checks.

Portion control is both an art and a science. It requires attention to detail, a bit of math, and ongoing adjustments based on your dog's unique needs. Think of it as crafting a bespoke diet plan for your furry friend, tailored to keep them in peak condition and full of life.

EASY AND DELICIOUS RECIPES

BAKED

CHICKEN AND VEGETABLE CASSEROLE

25% protein, 35% carbohydrates, 15% fat, 10% minerals, 7% fiber, 3% cholesterol, 3% sodium, 2% potassium
Total Calories: 550 kcal (0.67 kcal/g, 18.97 kcal/oz)
Total Recipe Amount: 29 oz (822 g)

INGREDIENTS

- 2 cups cooked chicken, shredded
- 1 cup chopped carrots
- 1 cup chopped green beans
- 1/2 cup peas
- 1 cup cooked brown rice
- 1/2 cup low sodium chicken broth

Prep. time: 15 min   Cook time: 45 min

DIRECTIONS

1. Preheat the oven to 350°F (175°C).
2. Combine all ingredients and mix thoroughly in a large bowl.
3. Transfer the mixture to a baking dish and spread evenly.
4. Bake in the preheated oven for 45 minutes or until heated through and vegetables are tender.
5. Let cool before serving.

CHICKEN AND GREEN BEAN COOKIES

22% protein, 35% carbohydrates, 12% fat, 10% minerals, 8% fiber, 5% cholesterol, 4% sodium, 3% potassium
Total Calories: 310 kcal (1.09 kcal/g, 31.0 kcal/oz)
Total Recipe Amount: 10 oz (283.5 g)

INGREDIENTS

- 1 cup cooked chicken breast, chopped
- 1/2 cup chopped green beans
- 1 egg
- 1/4 cup oat flour
- 1/4 cup rolled oats

Prep. time: 15 min   Cook time: 25 min

DIRECTIONS

1. Preheat your oven to 350°F (175°C).
2. Combine the chopped chicken, green beans, and egg in a large mixing bowl. Mix until well combined.
3. Gradually add the oat flour and rolled oats to the mixture, stirring until a dough forms.
4. Shape the mixture into cookie shapes and place them on a baking sheet lined with parchment paper.
5. Bake for 25 minutes or until the cookies are firm and slightly golden.

CHICKEN AND SWEET POTATO BITES

26% protein, 34% carbohydrates, 10% fat, 7% minerals, 5% fiber, 3% cholesterol, 8% sodium, 7% potassium
Total Calories: 350 kcal (1.23 kcal/g, 35.0 kcal/oz)
Total Recipe Amount: 10 oz (283.5 g)

INGREDIENTS

- 1 cup cooked chicken breast, chopped
- 1 cup cooked sweet potato, mashed
- 1 egg
- 1/2 cup oat flour

Prep. time: 15 min   Cook time: 30 min

DIRECTIONS

1. Preheat your oven to 350°F (175°C).
2. Combine the chopped chicken, mashed sweet potato, and egg in a mixing bowl. Mix until well combined.
3. Gradually add the oat flour to the mixture until it forms a dough-like consistency.
4. Roll the mixture into bite-sized balls and place them on a baking sheet lined with parchment paper.
5. Bake for 30 minutes or until the bites are firm and slightly golden.

CHICKEN AND APPLE MUFFINS

22% protein, 36% carbohydrates, 12% fat, 6% minerals, 5% fiber, 4% cholesterol, 7% sodium, 8% potassium
Total Calories: 400 kcal (1.41 kcal/g, 40.0 kcal/oz)
Total Recipe Amount: 10 oz (283.5 g)

INGREDIENTS

- 1 cup cooked chicken breast, chopped
- 1 cup applesauce (unsweetened)
- 1 egg
- 1/2 cup whole wheat flour
- 1/2 tsp baking powder

Prep. time: 10 min   Cook time: 25 min

DIRECTIONS

1. Preheat your oven to 350°F (175°C).
2. Combine the chopped chicken, applesauce, and egg in a mixing bowl. Mix until well combined.
3. Gradually add the whole wheat flour and baking powder to the mixture, stirring until it forms a batter.
4. Spoon the batter into a greased muffin tin, filling each cup about two-thirds full.
5. Bake for 25 minutes until the muffins are firm and slightly golden on top.

CHICKEN AND CARROT PATTIES

26% protein, 34% carbohydrates, 10% fat, 7% minerals, 5% fiber, 3% cholesterol, 8% sodium, 7% potassium
Total Calories: 380 kcal (1.34 kcal/g, 37.9 kcal/oz)
Total Recipe Amount: 10 oz (283.5 g)

INGREDIENTS

- 1 cup cooked chicken breast, chopped
- 1 cup grated carrots
- 1 egg
- 1/2 cup oat flour
- 1 tbsp olive oil

Prep. time: 15 min   Cook time: 20 min

DIRECTIONS

1. Preheat your oven to 350°F (175°C).
2. Combine the chopped chicken, grated carrots, and egg in a mixing bowl. Mix until well combined.
3. Gradually add the oat flour to the mixture until it forms a dough-like consistency.
4. Form the mixture into small patties and place them on a baking sheet lined with parchment paper.
5. Brush the patties with olive oil and bake for 20 minutes or until the patties are firm and slightly golden.

TURKEY AND CRANBERRY MEATBALLS

28% protein, 32% carbohydrates, 10% fat, 10% minerals, 5% fiber, 5% cholesterol, 5% sodium, 5% potassium
Total Calories: 350 kcal (1.24 kcal/g, 35.0 kcal/oz)
Total Recipe Amount: 10 oz (283.5 g)

INGREDIENTS

- 1 cup ground turkey
- 1/2 cup dried cranberries, chopped
- 1 egg
- 1/2 cup oat flour
- 1 tbsp olive oil

Prep. time: 15 min   Cook time: 20 min

DIRECTIONS

1. Preheat your oven to 350°F (175°C).
2. Combine the ground turkey, chopped cranberries, and egg in a mixing bowl. Mix until well combined.
3. Gradually add the oat flour to the mixture until it forms a dough-like consistency.
4. Form the mixture into small meatballs and place them on a baking sheet lined with parchment paper.
5. Brush the meatballs with olive oil and bake for 20 minutes or until the meatballs are firm and slightly golden.

TURKEY AND SPINACH LOAF

30% protein, 25% carbohydrates, 15% fat, 10% minerals, 7% fiber, 3% cholesterol, 5% sodium, 5% potassium
Total Calories: 370 kcal (1.30 kcal/g, 37.0 kcal/oz)
Total Recipe Amount: 10 oz (283.5 g)

INGREDIENTS

- 1 cup ground turkey
- 1 cup fresh spinach, chopped
- 1 egg
- 1/2 cup oat flour
- 1 tbsp olive oil

Prep. time: 15 min   Cook time: 30 min

DIRECTIONS

1. Preheat your oven to 350°F (175°C).
2. Combine the ground turkey, chopped spinach, and egg in a mixing bowl. Mix until well combined.
3. Gradually add the oat flour to the mixture until it forms a dough-like consistency.
4. Press the mixture into a greased loaf pan.
5. Bake for 30 minutes until the loaf is firm and slightly golden.

TURKEY AND BLUEBERRY CRISPS

24% protein, 35% carbohydrates, 12% fat, 10% minerals, 8% fiber, 5% cholesterol, 4% sodium, 2% potassium
Total Calories: 320 kcal (1.13 kcal/g, 32.0 kcal/oz)
Total Recipe Amount: 10 oz (283.5 g)

INGREDIENTS

- 1 cup cooked turkey breast, chopped
- 1/2 cup fresh blueberries
- 1 egg
- 1/4 cup oat flour
- 1/4 cup rolled oats

Prep. time: 15 min   Cook time: 25 min

DIRECTIONS

1. Preheat your oven to 350°F (175°C).
2. Combine the chopped turkey, blueberries, and egg in a large mixing bowl. Mix until well combined.
3. Gradually add the oat flour and rolled oats to the mixture, stirring until a dough forms.
4. Shape the mixture into thin crisps and place them on a baking sheet lined with parchment paper.
5. Bake for 25 minutes or until the crisps are firm and slightly golden.

TURKEY AND BANANA CRUNCHIES

20% protein, 35% carbohydrates, 15% fat, 12% minerals, 8% fiber, 5% cholesterol, 3% sodium, 2% potassium
Total Calories: 290 kcal (1.02 kcal/g, 29.0 kcal/oz)
Total Recipe Amount: 10 oz (283.5 g)

INGREDIENTS

- 1 cup cooked turkey breast, chopped
- 1/2 cup mashed banana
- 1 egg
- 1/4 cup oat flour
- 1/4 cup rolled oats

Prep. time: 15 min   Cook time: 25 min

DIRECTIONS

1. Preheat your oven to 350°F (175°C).
2. Combine the chopped turkey, mashed banana, and egg in a large mixing bowl. Mix until well combined.
3. Gradually add the oat flour and rolled oats to the mixture, stirring until a dough forms.
4. Shape the mixture into crunchies and place them on a baking sheet lined with parchment paper.
5. Bake for 25 minutes or until the crunchies are firm and slightly golden.

TURKEY AND PUMPKIN BISCUITS

28% protein, 32% carbohydrates, 15% fat, 10% minerals, 5% fiber, 3% cholesterol, 4% sodium, 3% potassium
Total Calories: 330 kcal (1.17 kcal/g, 33.0 kcal/oz)
Total Recipe Amount: 10 oz (283.5 g)

INGREDIENTS

- 1 cup cooked turkey, chopped
- 1 cup canned pumpkin (not pumpkin pie filling)
- 1 egg
- 1/2 cup oat flour

Prep. time: 15 min   Cook time: 30 min

DIRECTIONS

1. Preheat your oven to 350°F (175°C).
2. Combine the chopped turkey, canned pumpkin, and egg in a mixing bowl. Mix until well combined.
3. Gradually add the oat flour to the mixture until it forms a dough-like consistency.
4. Roll the mixture into small balls and flatten them into biscuit shapes on a baking sheet lined with parchment paper.
5. Bake for 30 minutes until the biscuits are firm and slightly golden.

DUCK AND SWEET POTATO CAKES

28% protein, 32% carbohydrates, 15% fat, 10% minerals, 7% fiber, 3% cholesterol, 3% sodium, 2% potassium
Total Calories: 360 kcal (1.27 kcal/g, 36.0 kcal/oz)
Total Recipe Amount: 10 oz (283.5 g)

INGREDIENTS

- 1 cup cooked duck, chopped
- 1 cup cooked sweet potato, mashed
- 1 egg
- 1/2 cup oat flour
- 1 tbsp olive oil

Prep. time: 15 min   Cook time: 20 min

DIRECTIONS

1. Preheat your oven to 350°F (175°C).
2. Combine the chopped duck, mashed sweet potato, and egg in a mixing bowl. Mix until well combined.
3. Gradually add the oat flour to the mixture until it forms a dough-like consistency.
4. Form the mixture into small cakes and place them on a baking sheet lined with parchment paper.
5. Brush the cakes with olive oil and bake for 20 minutes until the cakes are firm and slightly golden.

DUCK AND PEA MUFFINS

26% protein, 34% carbohydrates, 10% fat, 7% minerals, 5% fiber, 3% cholesterol, 8% sodium, 7% potassium
Total Calories: 350 kcal (1.24 kcal/g, 35.0 kcal/oz)
Total Recipe Amount: 10 oz (283.5 g)

INGREDIENTS

- 1 cup cooked duck, chopped
- 1 cup peas, mashed
- 1 egg
- 1/2 cup oat flour
- 1 tbsp olive oil

Prep. time: 15 min   Cook time: 25 min

DIRECTIONS

1. Preheat your oven to 350°F (175°C).
2. Combine the chopped duck, mashed peas, and egg in a mixing bowl. Mix until well combined.
3. Gradually add the oat flour to the mixture until it forms a batter-like consistency.
4. Spoon the mixture into a greased muffin tin, filling each cup about two-thirds full.
5. Bake for 25 minutes until the muffins are firm and slightly golden on top.

DUCK AND PUMPKIN BARS

28% protein, 30% carbohydrates, 15% fat, 10% minerals, 10% fiber, 3% cholesterol, 2% sodium, 2% potassium
Total Calories: 350 kcal (1.24 kcal/g, 35.0 kcal/oz)
Total Recipe Amount: 10 oz (283.5 g)

INGREDIENTS

- 1 cup cooked duck breast, chopped
- 1/2 cup pumpkin puree
- 1 egg
- 1/4 cup oat flour
- 1/4 cup rolled oats

Prep. time: 15 min   Cook time: 25 min

DIRECTIONS

1. Preheat your oven to 350°F (175°C).
2. Combine the chopped duck, pumpkin puree, and egg in a large mixing bowl. Mix until well combined.
3. Gradually add the oat flour and rolled oats to the mixture, stirring until a dough forms.
4. Press the mixture into a greased baking dish and bake for 25 minutes or until firm and golden.
5. Let cool, then cut into bars.

BEEF AND BROCCOLI BITES

30% protein, 30% carbohydrates, 15% fat, 10% minerals, 7% fiber, 3% cholesterol, 3% sodium, 2% potassium
Total Calories: 360 kcal (1.27 kcal/g, 36.0 kcal/oz)
Total Recipe Amount: 10 oz (283.5 g)

INGREDIENTS

- 1 cup cooked beef, chopped
- 1 cup broccoli, finely chopped
- 1 egg
- 1/2 cup oat flour
- 1 tbsp olive oil

Prep. time: 15 min   Cook time: 25 min

DIRECTIONS

1. Preheat your oven to 350°F (175°C).
2. Combine the chopped beef, finely chopped broccoli, and egg in a mixing bowl. Mix until well combined.
3. Gradually add the oat flour to the mixture until it forms a dough-like consistency.
4. Roll the mixture into small bite-sized balls and place them on a baking sheet lined with parchment paper.
5. Bake for 25 minutes until the bites are firm and slightly golden.

BEEF AND CARROT MUFFINS

28% protein, 32% carbohydrates, 15% fat, 10% minerals, 7% fiber, 3% cholesterol, 3% sodium, 2% potassium
Total Calories: 360 kcal (1.27 kcal/g, 36.0 kcal/oz)
Total Recipe Amount: 10 oz (283.5 g)

INGREDIENTS

- 1 cup cooked beef, chopped
- 1 cup grated carrots
- 1 egg
- 1/2 cup oat flour
- 1 tbsp olive oil

Prep. time: 15 min   Cook time: 25 min

DIRECTIONS

1. Preheat your oven to 350°F (175°C).
2. Combine the chopped beef, grated carrots, and egg in a mixing bowl. Mix until well combined.
3. Gradually add the oat flour to the mixture until it forms a batter-like consistency.
4. Spoon the mixture into a greased muffin tin, filling each cup about two-thirds full.
5. Bake for 25 minutes or until the muffins are firm and slightly golden on top.

BEEF AND CARROT CHIPS

24% protein, 34% carbohydrates, 12% fat, 10% minerals, 8% fiber, 5% cholesterol, 4% sodium, 2% potassium
Total Calories: 320 kcal (1.13 kcal/g, 32.0 kcal/oz)
Total Recipe Amount: 10 oz (283.5 g)

INGREDIENTS

- 1 cup cooked beef, chopped
- 1/2 cup grated carrot
- 1 egg
- 1/4 cup oat flour
- 1/4 cup rolled oats

Prep. time: 15 min   Cook time: 25 min

DIRECTIONS

1. Preheat your oven to 350°F (175°C).
2. Combine the chopped beef, grated carrot, and egg in a large mixing bowl. Mix until well combined.
3. Gradually add the oat flour and rolled oats to the mixture, stirring until a dough forms.
4. Shape the mixture into chip shapes and place them on a baking sheet lined with parchment paper.
5. Bake for 25 minutes or until the chips are firm and slightly golden.

BEEF AND ZUCCHINI PATTIES

26% protein, 34% carbohydrates, 10% fat, 7% minerals, 5% fiber, 3% cholesterol, 8% sodium, 7% potassium
Total Calories: 350 kcal (1.24 kcal/g, 35.0 kcal/oz)
Total Recipe Amount: 10 oz (283.5 g)

INGREDIENTS

- 1 cup cooked beef, chopped
- 1 cup grated zucchini
- 1 egg
- 1/2 cup oat flour
- 1 tbsp olive oil

Prep. time: 15 min   Cook time: 20 min

DIRECTIONS

1. Preheat your oven to 350°F (175°C).
2. Combine the chopped beef, grated zucchini, and egg in a mixing bowl. Mix until well combined.
3. Gradually add the oat flour to the mixture until it forms a dough-like consistency.
4. Form the mixture into small patties and place them on a baking sheet lined with parchment paper.
5. Bake for 20 minutes until the patties are firm and slightly golden.

PORK AND SWEET POTATO LOAF

28% protein, 32% carbohydrates, 15% fat, 10% minerals, 7% fiber, 3% cholesterol, 3% sodium, 2% potassium
Total Calories: 380 kcal (1.34 kcal/g, 38.0 kcal/oz)
Total Recipe Amount: 10 oz (283.5 g)

INGREDIENTS

- 1 cup cooked pork, chopped
- 1 cup cooked sweet potato, mashed
- 1 egg
- 1/2 cup oat flour
- 1 tbsp olive oil

Prep. time: 15 min   Cook time: 35 min

DIRECTIONS

1. Preheat your oven to 350°F (175°C).
2. Combine the chopped pork, mashed sweet potato, and egg in a mixing bowl. Mix until well combined.
3. Gradually add the oat flour to the mixture until it forms a dough-like consistency.
4. Press the mixture into a greased loaf pan.
5. Bake for 35 minutes until the loaf is firm and slightly golden.

PORK AND GREEN BEAN CAKES

26% protein, 34% carbohydrates, 10% fat, 7% minerals, 5% fiber, 3% cholesterol, 8% sodium, 7% potassium
Total Calories: 370 kcal (1.31 kcal/g, 37.0 kcal/oz)
Total Recipe Amount: 10 oz (283.5 g)

INGREDIENTS

- 1 cup cooked pork, chopped
- 1 cup green beans, finely chopped
- 1 egg
- 1/2 cup oat flour
- 1 tbsp olive oil

Prep. time: 15 min   Cook time: 20 min

DIRECTIONS

1. Preheat your oven to 350°F (175°C).
2. Combine the chopped pork, finely chopped green beans, and egg in a mixing bowl. Mix until well combined.
3. Gradually add the oat flour to the mixture until it forms a dough-like consistency.
4. Form the mixture into small cakes and place them on a baking sheet lined with parchment paper.
5. Bake for 20 minutes until the cakes are firm and slightly golden.

PORK AND APPLE BISCUITS

28% protein, 32% carbohydrates, 15% fat, 10% minerals, 7% fiber, 3% cholesterol, 3% sodium, 2% potassium
Total Calories: 360 kcal (1.27 kcal/g, 36.0 kcal/oz)
Total Recipe Amount: 10 oz (283.5 g)

INGREDIENTS

- 1 cup cooked pork, chopped
- 1 cup grated apple
- 1 egg
- 1/2 cup oat flour
- 1 tbsp olive oil

Prep. time: 15 min   Cook time: 25 min

DIRECTIONS

1. Preheat your oven to 350°F (175°C).
2. Combine the chopped pork, grated apple, and egg in a mixing bowl. Mix until well combined.
3. Gradually add the oat flour to the mixture until it forms a dough-like consistency.
4. Roll the mixture into small balls and flatten them into biscuit shapes on a baking sheet lined with parchment paper.
5. Bake for 25 minutes until the biscuits are firm and slightly golden.

PORK AND PUMPKIN ROUNDS

22% protein, 35% carbohydrates, 12% fat, 10% minerals, 8% fiber, 5% cholesterol, 4% sodium, 3% potassium
Total Calories: 310 kcal (1.09 kcal/g, 31.0 kcal/oz)
Total Recipe Amount: 10 oz (283.5 g)

INGREDIENTS

- 1 cup cooked pork, chopped
- 1/2 cup pumpkin puree
- 1 egg
- 1/4 cup oat flour
- 1/4 cup rolled oats

Prep. time: 15 min   Cook time: 25 min

DIRECTIONS

1. Preheat your oven to 350°F (175°C).
2. Combine the chopped pork, pumpkin puree, and egg in a large mixing bowl. Mix until well combined.
3. Gradually add the oat flour and rolled oats to the mixture, stirring until a dough forms.
4. Shape the mixture into rounds and place them on a baking sheet lined with parchment paper.
5. Bake for 25 minutes or until the rounds are firm and slightly golden.

PORK AND PEAR STICKS

25% protein, 30% carbohydrates, 15% fat, 10% minerals, 8% fiber, 5% cholesterol, 5% sodium, 2% potassium
Total Calories: 360 kcal (1.27 kcal/g, 36.0 kcal/oz)
Total Recipe Amount: 10 oz (283.5 g)

INGREDIENTS

- 1 cup cooked pork, chopped
- 1/2 cup grated pear
- 1 egg
- 1/4 cup oat flour
- 1/4 cup rolled oats

Prep. time: 15 min   Cook time: 30 min

DIRECTIONS

1. Preheat your oven to 350°F (175°C).
2. Combine the chopped pork, grated pear, and egg in a large mixing bowl. Mix until well combined.
3. Gradually add the oat flour and rolled oats to the mixture, stirring until a dough forms.
4. Shape the mixture into thin sticks and place them on a baking sheet lined with parchment paper.
5. Bake for 30 minutes or until the sticks are firm and slightly golden.

FISH AND ASPARAGUS QUICHE

30% protein, 30% carbohydrates, 15% fat, 10% minerals, 7% fiber, 3% cholesterol, 3% sodium, 2% potassium
Total Calories: 400 kcal (1.41 kcal/g, 40 kcal/oz)
Total Recipe Amount: 10 oz (283.5 g)

INGREDIENTS

- 1 cup cooked white fish, flaked
- 1 cup asparagus, chopped
- 2 eggs
- 1/2 cup oat flour
- 1/4 cup plain yogurt

Prep. time: 20 min   Cook time: 30 min

DIRECTIONS

1. Preheat your oven to 350°F (175°C).
2. Combine the flaked white fish, chopped asparagus, and eggs in a mixing bowl. Mix until well combined.
3. Gradually add the oat flour and plain yogurt to the mixture until it forms a batter-like consistency.
4. Pour the mixture into a greased quiche dish or pie pan.
5. Bake for 30 minutes until the quiche is firm and slightly golden on top.

SALMON AND SWEET POTATO SQUARES

22% protein, 40% carbohydrates, 12% fat, 8% minerals, 10% fiber, 3% cholesterol, 3% sodium, 2% potassium
Total Calories: 330 kcal (1.16 kcal/g, 33.0 kcal/oz)
Total Recipe Amount: 10 oz (283.5 g)

INGREDIENTS

- 1 cup cooked salmon, flaked
- 1/2 cup cooked sweet potato, mashed
- 1 egg
- 1/4 cup oat flour
- 1/4 cup rolled oats

Prep. time: 15 min   Cook time: 25 min

DIRECTIONS

1. Preheat your oven to 350°F (175°C).
2. Combine the flaked salmon, mashed sweet potato, and egg in a large mixing bowl. Mix until well combined.
3. Gradually add the oat flour and rolled oats to the mixture, stirring until a dough forms.
4. Press the mixture into a greased baking dish and bake for 25 minutes or until firm and golden.
5. Let cool, then cut into squares.

WHITE FISH AND CARROT CRUNCHIES

24% protein, 34% carbohydrates, 12% fat, 10% minerals, 8% fiber, 5% cholesterol, 4% sodium, 2% potassium
Total Calories: 320 kcal (1.13 kcal/g, 32.0 kcal/oz)
Total Recipe Amount: 10 oz (283.5 g)

INGREDIENTS

- 1 cup cooked white fish, chopped
- 1/2 cup grated carrot
- 1 egg
- 1/4 cup oat flour
- 1/4 cup rolled oats

Prep. time: 15 min   Cook time: 25 min

DIRECTIONS

1. Preheat your oven to 350°F (175°C).
2. Combine the chopped fish, grated carrot, and egg in a large mixing bowl. Mix until well combined.
3. Gradually add the oat flour and rolled oats to the mixture, stirring until a dough forms.
4. Shape the mixture into crunchies and place them on a baking sheet lined with parchment paper.
5. Bake for 25 minutes or until the crunchies are firm and slightly golden.

WHITE FISH AND SWEET CORN DROPS

20% protein, 35% carbohydrates, 15% fat, 12% minerals, 8% fiber, 5% cholesterol, 3% sodium, 2% potassium
Total Calories: 290 kcal (1.02 kcal/g, 29.0 kcal/oz)
Total Recipe Amount: 10 oz (283.5 g)

INGREDIENTS

- 1 cup cooked white fish, chopped
- 1/2 cup sweet corn kernels
- 1 egg
- 1/4 cup oat flour
- 1/4 cup rolled oats

Prep. time: 15 min   Cook time: 25 min

DIRECTIONS

1. Preheat your oven to 350°F (175°C).
2. Combine the chopped fish, sweet corn, and egg in a large mixing bowl. Mix until well combined.
3. Gradually add the oat flour and rolled oats to the mixture, stirring until a dough forms.
4. Shape the mixture into drop shapes and place them on a baking sheet lined with parchment paper.
5. Bake for 25 minutes or until the drops are firm and slightly golden.

WHITE FISH AND PEA PATTIES

28% protein, 32% carbohydrates, 15% fat, 10% minerals, 7% fiber, 3% cholesterol, 3% sodium, 2% potassium
Total Calories: 340 kcal (1.20 kcal/g, 34.0 kcal/oz)
Total Recipe Amount: 10 oz (283.5 g)

INGREDIENTS

- 1 cup cooked white fish, flaked
- 1 cup cooked peas, mashed
- 1 egg
- 1/2 cup oat flour
- 1 tbsp olive oil

Prep. time: 15 min   Cook time: 20 min

DIRECTIONS

1. Preheat your oven to 350°F (175°C).
2. Combine the flaked white fish, mashed peas, and egg in a mixing bowl. Mix until well combined.
3. Gradually add the oat flour to the mixture until it forms a dough-like consistency.
4. Form the mixture into small patties and place them on a baking sheet lined with parchment paper.
5. Bake for 20 minutes until the patties are firm and slightly golden.

LIVER AND PUMPKIN MUFFINS

30% protein, 30% carbohydrates, 15% fat, 10% minerals, 7% fiber, 3% cholesterol, 3% sodium, 2% potassium
Total Calories: 380 kcal (1.34 kcal/g, 38.0 kcal/oz)
Total Recipe Amount: 10 oz (283.5 g)

INGREDIENTS

- 1 cup cooked liver, chopped
- 1 cup cooked pumpkin puree
- 1 egg
- 1/2 cup oat flour
- 1 tbsp olive oil

Prep. time: 15 min   Cook time: 25 min

DIRECTIONS

1. Preheat your oven to 350°F (175°C).
2. Combine the chopped liver, pumpkin puree, and egg in a mixing bowl. Mix until well combined.
3. Gradually add the oat flour to the mixture until it forms a batter-like consistency.
4. Spoon the mixture into a greased muffin tin, filling each cup about two-thirds full.
5. Bake for 25 minutes until the muffins are firm and slightly golden on top.

KIDNEY AND SWEET POTATO PATTIES

30% protein, 30% carbohydrates, 15% fat, 10% minerals, 7% fiber, 3% cholesterol, 3% sodium, 2% potassium
Total Calories: 380 kcal (1.34 kcal/g, 38.0 kcal/oz)
Total Recipe Amount: 10 oz (283.5 g)

INGREDIENTS

- 1 cup cooked kidney, finely chopped
- 1 cup mashed sweet potato
- 1 egg
- 1/2 cup oat flour
- 1 tbsp olive oil

Prep. time: 15 min   Cook time: 20 min

DIRECTIONS

1. Preheat your oven to 350°F (175°C).
2. Combine the chopped kidney, mashed sweet potato, and egg in a mixing bowl. Mix until well combined.
3. Gradually add the oat flour to the mixture until it forms a dough-like consistency.
4. Form the mixture into small patties and place them on a baking sheet lined with parchment paper.
5. Bake for 20 minutes until the patties are firm and slightly golden.

HEART ROLL WITH PINEAPPLE

30% protein, 25% carbohydrates, 15% fat, 8% minerals, 7% fiber, 5% cholesterol, 5% sodium, 5% potassium
Total Calories: 350 kcal (1.24 kcal/g, 35.0 kcal/oz)
Total Recipe Amount: 10 oz (283.5 g)

INGREDIENTS

- 1 cup cooked chicken hearts, chopped
- 1/2 cup fresh pineapple, chopped
- 1 egg
- 1/4 cup oat flour
- 1/4 cup rolled oats

Prep. time: 20 min   Cook time: 35 min

DIRECTIONS

1. Preheat your oven to 350°F (175°C).
2. Combine the chopped chicken hearts, pineapple, and egg in a large mixing bowl. Mix until well combined.
3. Gradually add the oat flour and rolled oats to the mixture, stirring until a dough forms.
4. Shape the mixture into a roll and place it on a baking sheet lined with parchment paper.
5. Bake for 35 minutes or until the roll is firm and slightly golden. Let it cool before slicing.

HEART AND CARROT BISCUITS

28% protein, 32% carbohydrates, 15% fat, 10% minerals, 7% fiber, 3% cholesterol, 3% sodium, 2% potassium
Total Calories: 400 kcal (1.41 kcal/g, 40.0 kcal/oz)
Total Recipe Amount: 10 oz (283.5 g)

INGREDIENTS

- 1 cup cooked beef heart, finely chopped
- 1 cup grated carrots
- 1 egg
- 1/2 cup oat flour
- 1 tbsp olive oil

Prep. time: 20 min   Cook time: 30 min

DIRECTIONS

1. Preheat your oven to 350°F (175°C).
2. Combine the chopped beef heart, grated carrots, and egg in a mixing bowl. Mix until well combined.
3. Gradually add the oat flour to the mixture until it forms a dough-like consistency.
4. Roll the mixture into small balls and flatten them into biscuit shapes on a baking sheet lined with parchment paper.
5. Bake for 30 minutes until the biscuits are firm and slightly golden.

RABBIT AND BLUEBERRY BISCUITS

28% protein, 32% carbohydrates, 15% fat, 10% minerals, 7% fiber, 3% cholesterol, 3% sodium, 2% potassium
Total Calories: 360 kcal (1.27 kcal/g, 36.0 kcal/oz)
Total Recipe Amount: 10 oz (283.5 g)

INGREDIENTS

- 1 cup cooked rabbit meat, finely chopped
- 1/2 cup fresh blueberries
- 1 egg
- 1/2 cup oat flour
- 1 tbsp olive oil

Prep. time: 20 min   Cook time: 30 min

DIRECTIONS

1. Preheat your oven to 350°F (175°C).
2. Combine the chopped rabbit meat, blueberries, and egg in a mixing bowl. Mix until well combined.
3. Gradually add the oat flour to the mixture until it forms a dough-like consistency.
4. Roll the mixture into small balls and flatten them into biscuit shapes on a baking sheet lined with parchment paper.
5. Bake for 30 minutes until the biscuits are firm and slightly golden.

RABBIT AND CARROT LOAF

30% protein, 30% carbohydrates, 15% fat, 10% minerals, 7% fiber, 3% cholesterol, 3% sodium, 2% potassium
Total Calories: 400 kcal (1.41 kcal/g, 40.0 kcal/oz)
Total Recipe Amount: 10 oz (283.5 g)

INGREDIENTS

- 1 cup cooked rabbit meat, finely chopped
- 1/2 cup grated carrots
- 1 egg
- 1/2 cup oat flour
- 1 tbsp olive oil

Prep. time: 20 min   Cook time: 40 min

DIRECTIONS

1. Preheat your oven to 350°F (175°C).
2. Combine the chopped rabbit meat, grated carrots, and egg in a mixing bowl. Mix until well combined.
3. Gradually add the oat flour to the mixture until it forms a batter-like consistency.
4. Grease a small loaf pan and pour the mixture into the pan, spreading it evenly.
5. Bake for 40 minutes until the loaf is firm and golden brown.

RABBIT AND WATERMELON SQUARES

22% protein, 40% carbohydrates, 10% fat, 10% minerals, 8% fiber, 4% cholesterol, 3% sodium, 3% potassium
Total Calories: 300 kcal (1.06 kcal/g, 30.0 kcal/oz)
Total Recipe Amount: 10 oz (283.5 g)

INGREDIENTS

- 1 cup cooked rabbit, chopped
- 1/2 cup watermelon, chopped
- 1 egg
- 1/4 cup oat flour
- 1/4 cup rolled oats

Prep. time: 15 min   Cook time: 25 min

DIRECTIONS

1. Preheat your oven to 350°F (175°C).
2. In a large mixing bowl, combine the chopped rabbit, watermelon, and egg. Mix until well combined.
3. Gradually add the oat flour and rolled oats to the mixture, stirring until a dough forms.
4. Press the mixture into a greased baking dish and bake for 25 minutes or until firm and golden.
5. Let cool, then cut into squares.

LAMB AND PEACH BARS

25% protein, 30% carbohydrates, 12% fat, 10% minerals, 10% fiber, 3% cholesterol, 5% sodium, 5% potassium
Total Calories: 320 kcal (1.13 kcal/g, 32.0 kcal/oz)
Total Recipe Amount: 10 oz (283.5 g)

INGREDIENTS

- 1 cup cooked lamb, chopped
- 1/2 cup fresh peaches, chopped
- 1 egg
- 1/4 cup oat flour
- 1/4 cup rolled oats

Prep. time: 15 min   Cook time: 25 min

DIRECTIONS

1. Preheat your oven to 350°F (175°C).
2. Combine the chopped lamb, peaches, and egg in a large mixing bowl. Mix until well combined.
3. Gradually add the oat flour and rolled oats to the mixture, stirring until a dough forms.
4. Press the mixture into a greased baking dish and bake for 25 minutes or until firm and golden.
5. Let cool, then cut into bars.

LAMB AND SWEET POTATO PATTIES

30% protein, 30% carbohydrates, 15% fat, 10% minerals, 7% fiber, 3% cholesterol, 3% sodium, 2% potassium
Total Calories: 520 kcal (1.84 kcal/g, 52.0 kcal/oz)
Total Recipe Amount: 10 oz (283.5 g)

INGREDIENTS

- 1 cup ground lamb
- 1 cup mashed sweet potatoes
- 1/4 cup oat flour
- 1 egg
- 1 tbsp olive oil

Prep. time: 20 min   Cook time: 20 min

DIRECTIONS

1. Preheat your oven to 350°F (175°C).
2. Combine the ground lamb, mashed sweet potatoes, oat flour, and egg in a mixing bowl. Mix until well combined.
3. Form the mixture into small patties about 2 inches in diameter.
4. Heat the olive oil in a skillet over medium heat. Cook each side of the patties for about 3 minutes until browned.
5. Transfer the patties to a baking sheet and bake for 15 minutes or until fully cooked.

LAMB AND GREEN BEAN MUFFINS

26% protein, 34% carbohydrates, 10% fat, 7% minerals, 5% fiber, 3% cholesterol, 8% sodium, 7% potassium
Total Calories: 600 kcal (1.90 kcal/g, 54 kcal/oz)
Total Recipe Amount: 11 oz (315 g)

INGREDIENTS

- 1 cup ground lamb
- 1/2 cup finely chopped green beans
- 1/2 cup rolled oats
- 1/4 cup grated carrots
- 2 eggs
- 1/4 cup plain yogurt

Prep. time: 15 min   Cook time: 25 min

DIRECTIONS

1. Preheat the oven to 350°F (175°C). Grease a muffin tin or line it with muffin cups.
2. Combine the ground lamb, green beans, oats, grated carrots, eggs, and yogurt in a large bowl. Mix until well combined.
3. Spoon the mixture into the muffin cups, filling each about three-quarters full.
4. Bake for 25 minutes or until a toothpick inserted into the center comes clean.
5. Let the muffins cool completely before serving.

LAMB AND BANANA STRIPS

26% protein, 34% carbohydrates, 12% fat, 10% minerals, 8% fiber, 4% cholesterol, 4% sodium, 2% potassium
Total Calories: 330 kcal (1.16 kcal/g, 33.0 kcal/oz)
Total Recipe Amount: 10 oz (283.5 g)

INGREDIENTS

- 1 cup cooked lamb, chopped
- 1/2 cup banana, mashed
- 1 egg
- 1/4 cup oat flour
- 1/4 cup rolled oats

Prep. time: 15 min   Cook time: 30 min

DIRECTIONS

1. Preheat your oven to 350°F (175°C).
2. Combine the chopped lamb, mashed banana, and egg in a large mixing bowl. Mix until well combined.
3. Gradually add the oat flour and rolled oats to the mixture, stirring until a dough forms.
4. Shape the mixture into thin strips and place them on a baking sheet lined with parchment paper.
5. Bake for 30 minutes or until the strips are firm and slightly golden.

LAMB AND PUMPKIN COOKIES

22% protein, 35% carbohydrates, 12% fat, 10% minerals, 8% fiber, 5% cholesterol, 4% sodium, 3% potassium
Total Calories: 310 kcal (1.09 kcal/g, 31.0 kcal/oz)
Total Recipe Amount: 10 oz (283.5 g)

INGREDIENTS

- 1 cup cooked lamb, chopped
- 1/2 cup pumpkin puree
- 1 egg
- 1/4 cup oat flour
- 1/4 cup rolled oats

Prep. time: 15 min   Cook time: 25 min

DIRECTIONS

1. Preheat your oven to 350°F (175°C).
2. Combine the chopped lamb, pumpkin puree, and egg in a large mixing bowl. Mix until well combined.
3. Gradually add the oat flour and rolled oats to the mixture, stirring until a dough forms.
4. Shape the mixture into cookie shapes and place them on a baking sheet lined with parchment paper.
5. Bake for 25 minutes or until the cookies are firm and slightly golden.

LAMB AND RICE CRISPS

22% protein, 34% carbohydrates, 12% fat, 10% minerals, 8% fiber, 5% cholesterol, 4% sodium, 3% potassium
Total Calories: 320 kcal (1.13 kcal/g, 32.0 kcal/oz)
Total Recipe Amount: 10 oz (283.5 g)

INGREDIENTS

- 1 cup cooked lamb, chopped
- 1/2 cup cooked brown rice
- 1 egg
- 1/4 cup oat flour
- 1/4 cup rolled oats

Prep. time: 15 min   Cook time: 25 min

DIRECTIONS

1. Preheat your oven to 350°F (175°C).
2. Combine the chopped lamb, cooked rice, and egg in a large mixing bowl. Mix until well combined.
3. Gradually add the oat flour and rolled oats to the mixture, stirring until a dough forms.
4. Shape the mixture into crisp shapes and place them on a baking sheet lined with parchment paper.
5. Bake for 25 minutes or until the crisps are firm and slightly golden.

LAMB AND BLUEBERRY BITS

24% protein, 35% carbohydrates, 12% fat, 10% minerals, 8% fiber, 5% cholesterol, 4% sodium, 2% potassium
Total Calories: 320 kcal (1.13 kcal/g, 32.0 kcal/oz)
Total Recipe Amount: 10 oz (283.5 g)

INGREDIENTS

- 1 cup cooked lamb, chopped
- 1/2 cup fresh blueberries
- 1 egg
- 1/4 cup oat flour
- 1/4 cup rolled oats

Prep. time: 15 min   Cook time: 25 min

DIRECTIONS

1. Preheat your oven to 350°F (175°C).
2. Combine the chopped lamb, blueberries, and egg in a large mixing bowl. Mix until well combined.
3. Gradually add the oat flour and rolled oats to the mixture, stirring until a dough forms.
4. Shape the mixture into bite-sized bits and place them on a baking sheet lined with parchment paper.
5. Bake for 25 minutes or until the bits are firm and slightly golden.

VENISON AND CARROT MUFFINS

26% protein, 34% carbohydrates, 10% fat, 7% minerals, 5% fiber, 3% cholesterol, 8% sodium, 7% potassium
Total Calories: 350 kcal (1.24 kcal/g, 35.0 kcal/oz)
Total Recipe Amount: 10 oz (283.5 g)

INGREDIENTS

- 1 cup ground venison
- 1/2 cup grated carrots
- 1/2 cup whole wheat flour
- 1/4 cup rolled oats
- 1/2 cup unsweetened applesauce
- 1 large egg

Prep. time: 15 min   Cook time: 25 min

DIRECTIONS

1. Preheat the oven to 350°F (175°C) and line a muffin tin with paper liners.
2. Combine ground venison, grated carrots, whole wheat flour, rolled oats, applesauce, and the egg in a mixing bowl. Mix well until all ingredients are fully incorporated.
3. Spoon the mixture into the muffin tin, filling each liner about 3/4 full.
4. Bake for 25 minutes or until a toothpick inserted into the center of a muffin comes out clean. Allow muffins to cool before serving.

VENISON AND BLUEBERRY STRIPS

24% protein, 35% carbohydrates, 12% fat, 10% minerals, 8% fiber, 5% cholesterol, 3% sodium, 3% potassium
Total Calories: 320 kcal (1.13 kcal/g, 32.0 kcal/oz)
Total Recipe Amount: 10 oz (283.5 g)

INGREDIENTS

- 1 cup cooked venison, chopped
- 1/4 cup fresh blueberries
- 1 egg
- 1/4 cup oat flour
- 1/4 cup rolled oats

Prep. time: 15 min   Cook time: 30 min

DIRECTIONS

1. Preheat your oven to 350°F (175°C).
2. Combine the chopped venison, blueberries, and egg in a large mixing bowl. Mix until well combined.
3. Gradually add the oat flour and rolled oats to the mixture, stirring until a dough forms.
4. Shape the mixture into thin strips and place them on a baking sheet lined with parchment paper.
5. Bake for 30 minutes or until the strips are firm and slightly golden.

VENISON AND SWEET POTATO PATTIES

30% protein, 35% carbohydrates, 12% fat, 6% minerals, 6% fiber, 2% cholesterol, 5% sodium, 4% potassium
Total Calories: 400 kcal (1.42 kcal/g, 40.3 kcal/oz)
Total Recipe Amount: 9.93 oz (282 g)

INGREDIENTS

- 1 cup ground venison
- 1 cup mashed sweet potatoes
- 1 egg
- 1/4 cup rolled oats
- 1/4 cup finely chopped spinach

Prep. time: 15 min   Cook time: 25 min

DIRECTIONS

1. Preheat the oven to 350°F.
2. Mix the ground venison, mashed sweet potatoes, egg, rolled oats, and chopped spinach until well combined in a large bowl.
3. Form the mixture into small patties and place them on a baking sheet lined with parchment paper.
4. Bake for 25 minutes or until the patties are cooked and slightly browned.

VENISON AND PUMPKIN BISCUITS

28% protein, 32% carbohydrates, 15% fat, 10% minerals, 7% fiber, 3% cholesterol, 3% sodium, 2% potassium
Total Calories: 360 kcal (1.27 kcal/g, 36.2 kcal/oz)
Total Recipe Amount: 10 oz (283.5 g)

INGREDIENTS

- 1 cup ground venison
- 1/2 cup pumpkin puree
- 1 egg
- 1/2 cup oat flour
- 1 tbsp coconut oil
- 1/2 tsp turmeric (optional, for added health benefits)

Prep. time: 15 min   Cook time: 30 min

DIRECTIONS

1. Preheat the oven to 350°F (175°C).
2. Mix the ground venison, pumpkin puree, egg, and coconut oil in a large bowl.
3. Gradually add the oat flour, mixing until a dough forms.
4. Roll out the dough on a lightly floured surface to about 1/4 inch thickness. Cut into desired shapes.
5. Place the biscuits on a baking sheet lined with parchment paper and bake for 30 minutes until golden brown.

VENISON AND SWEET POTATO NIBBLES

22% protein, 35% carbohydrates, 12% fat, 10% minerals, 8% fiber, 5% cholesterol, 4% sodium, 3% potassium
Total Calories: 310 kcal (1.09 kcal/g, 31.0 kcal/oz)
Total Recipe Amount: 10 oz (283.5 g)

INGREDIENTS

- 1 cup cooked venison, chopped
- 1/2 cup mashed sweet potato
- 1 egg
- 1/4 cup oat flour
- 1/4 cup rolled oats

Prep. time: 15 min   Cook time: 25 min

DIRECTIONS

1. Preheat your oven to 350°F (175°C).
2. Combine the chopped venison, mashed sweet potato, and egg in a large mixing bowl. Mix until well combined.
3. Gradually add the oat flour and rolled oats to the mixture, stirring until a dough forms.
4. Shape the mixture into nibble shapes and place them on a baking sheet lined with parchment paper.
5. Bake for 25 minutes or until the nibbles are firm and slightly golden.

SWEET POTATO AND PARSLEY BISCUITS

20% protein, 35% carbohydrates, 15% fat, 12% minerals, 8% fiber, 5% cholesterol, 3% sodium, 2% potassium
Total Calories: 290 kcal (1.02 kcal/g, 29.0 kcal/oz)
Total Recipe Amount: 10 oz (283.5 g)

INGREDIENTS

- 1 cup mashed sweet potato
- 1/2 cup chopped fresh parsley
- 1 egg
- 1/4 cup oat flour
- 1/4 cup rolled oats

Prep. time: 15 min   Cook time: 25 min

DIRECTIONS

1. Preheat your oven to 350°F (175°C).
2. Combine the mashed sweet potato, chopped parsley, and egg in a large mixing bowl. Mix until well combined.
3. Gradually add the oat flour and rolled oats to the mixture, stirring until a dough forms.
4. Shape the mixture into biscuit shapes and place them on a baking sheet lined with parchment paper.
5. Bake for 25 minutes or until the biscuits are firm and slightly golden.

SPINACH AND APPLE TREATS

22% protein, 34% carbohydrates, 12% fat, 10% minerals, 8% fiber, 5% cholesterol, 4% sodium, 3% potassium
Total Calories: 320 kcal (1.13 kcal/g, 32.0 kcal/oz)
Total Recipe Amount: 10 oz (283.5 g)

INGREDIENTS

- 1 cup chopped fresh spinach
- 1/2 cup grated apple
- 1 egg
- 1/4 cup oat flour
- 1/4 cup rolled oats

Prep. time: 15 min   Cook time: 25 min

DIRECTIONS

1. Preheat your oven to 350°F (175°C).
2. Combine the chopped spinach, grated apple, and egg in a large mixing bowl. Mix until well combined.
3. Gradually add the oat flour and rolled oats to the mixture, stirring until a dough forms.
4. Shape the mixture into treat shapes and place them on a baking sheet lined with parchment paper.
5. Bake for 25 minutes or until the treats are firm and slightly golden.

BANANA AND FLAXSEED SNACKS

20% protein, 35% carbohydrates, 15% fat, 10% minerals, 8% fiber, 5% cholesterol, 3% sodium, 4% potassium
Total Calories: 290 kcal (1.02 kcal/g, 29.0 kcal/oz)
Total Recipe Amount: 10 oz (283.5 g)

INGREDIENTS

- 1 cup mashed banana
- 1/4 cup flaxseed meal
- 1 egg
- 1/4 cup oat flour
- 1/4 cup rolled oats

Prep. time: 15 min   Cook time: 25 min

DIRECTIONS

1. Preheat your oven to 350°F (175°C).
2. Combine the mashed banana, flaxseed meal, and egg in a large mixing bowl. Mix until well combined.
3. Gradually add the oat flour and rolled oats to the mixture, stirring until a dough forms.
4. Shape the mixture into snack shapes and place them on a baking sheet lined with parchment paper.
5. Bake for 25 minutes or until the snacks are firm and slightly golden.

PUMPKIN AND CARROT BISCUITS

18% protein, 55% carbohydrates, 7% fat, 6% minerals, 7% fiber, 2% cholesterol, 3% sodium, 2% potassium
Total Calories: 300 kcal (1.06 kcal/g, 30.0 kcal/oz)
Total Recipe Amount: 10 oz (283 g)

INGREDIENTS

- 1 cup pumpkin puree
- 1/2 cup grated carrots
- 1 egg
- 2 cups whole wheat flour
- 1/4 cup water (as needed)

Prep. time: 15 min   Cook time: 25 min

DIRECTIONS

1. Preheat your oven to 350°F (175°C) and line a baking sheet with parchment paper.
2. Mix the pumpkin puree, grated carrots, and egg in a large bowl until well combined.
3. Gradually add the whole wheat flour, mixing until a dough forms. Add water to achieve the right consistency.
4. Roll out the dough on a lightly floured surface and cut it into shapes using a cookie cutter.
5. Place the biscuits on the prepared baking sheet and bake for 25 minutes until firm and golden brown.

SPINACH AND CARROT FRITTATA

25% protein, 20% carbohydrates, 30% fat, 8% minerals, 5% fiber, 3% cholesterol, 5% sodium, 4% potassium
Total Calories: 600 kcal (1.2 kcal/g, 34.0 kcal/oz)
Total Recipe Amount: 17.6 oz (500 g)

INGREDIENTS

- 1/2 cup fresh spinach, chopped
- 1/2 cup grated carrots
- 4 large eggs
- 1/4 cup low-fat milk
- 1 tbsp olive oil
- 1/4 tsp salt

Prep. time: 10 min   Cook time: 20 min

DIRECTIONS

1. Preheat the oven to 350°F.
2. Whisk together the eggs, milk, and salt in a bowl.
3. Stir in the spinach and grated carrots until well combined.
4. Heat olive oil in a skillet over medium heat, then pour the egg mixture.
5. Cook for about 5 minutes on the stovetop, then transfer the skillet to the oven and bake for 15 minutes or until the frittata is fully set and golden brown.

PEANUT BUTTER AND BANANA MUFFINS

12% protein, 48% carbohydrates, 22% fat, 6% minerals, 6% fiber, 2% cholesterol, 2% sodium, 2% potassium
Total Calories: 350 kcal (1.02 kcal/g, 42.0 kcal/oz)
Total Recipe Amount: 8.3 oz (343 g)

INGREDIENTS

- 1 cup whole wheat flour
- 1/2 cup rolled oats
- 1/2 cup peanut butter (unsalted, xylitol-free)
- 1 ripe banana, mashed
- 1 egg
- 1/2 cup water

Prep. time: 10 min   Cook time: 20 min

DIRECTIONS

1. Preheat your oven to 350°F (175°C) and line a muffin tin with paper liners.
2. Mix the whole wheat flour and rolled oats in a large bowl.
3. Combine the peanut butter, mashed banana, egg, and water in another bowl until smooth.
4. Add the wet ingredients to the dry ingredients and mix until just combined.
5. Spoon the batter into the muffin tin, filling each liner about two-thirds. Bake for 20 minutes or until a toothpick inserted into the center of a muffin comes out clean.

NO-BAKE

CHICKEN AND CARROT BITES

28% protein, 32% carbohydrates, 12% fat, 7% minerals, 8% fiber, 3% cholesterol, 5% sodium, 5% potassium
Total Calories: 300 kcal (1.06 kcal/g, 30.0 kcal/oz)
Total Recipe Amount: 10 oz (283.5 g)

INGREDIENTS

- 1 cup cooked, shredded chicken
- 1/2 cup grated carrots
- 1/2 cup rolled oats
- 1/4 cup unsweetened applesauce
- 2 tbsp peanut butter (unsalted, xylitol-free)

Prep. time: 15 min   Cook time: 0 min

DIRECTIONS

1. Combine all ingredients in a large bowl and mix until well combined.
2. Roll the mixture into small bite-sized balls.
3. Place the bites on a tray and refrigerate for at least 1 hour before serving.

CHICKEN AND PUMPKIN BALLS

24% protein, 30% carbohydrates, 15% fat, 10% minerals, 6% fiber, 5% cholesterol, 5% sodium, 5% potassium
Total Calories: 340 kcal (1.20 kcal/g, 34.0 kcal/oz)
Total Recipe Amount: 10 oz (283.5 g)

INGREDIENTS

- 1 cup cooked, shredded chicken
- 1/2 cup canned pumpkin (not pumpkin pie filling)
- 1/2 cup rolled oats
- 1/4 cup natural peanut butter (unsalted, xylitol-free)

Prep. time: 15 min   Cook time: 0 min

DIRECTIONS

1. Combine the cooked shredded chicken, canned pumpkin, rolled oats, and natural peanut butter in a large bowl. Mix until all ingredients are well blended.
2. Form the mixture into small balls about 1 inch in diameter.
3. Place the balls on a baking sheet lined with parchment paper.
4. Refrigerate the balls for at least 1 hour to firm up before serving.

CHICKEN AND SPINACH TREATS

28% protein, 32% carbohydrates, 12% fat, 7% minerals, 8% fiber, 3% cholesterol, 5% sodium, 5% potassium
Total Calories: 310 kcal (1.10 kcal/g, 31.2 kcal/oz)
Total Recipe Amount: 10 oz (283.5 g)

INGREDIENTS

- 1 cup cooked chicken breast, finely chopped
- 1/2 cup cooked spinach, finely chopped
- 1/2 cup rolled oats
- 1/4 cup pumpkin puree
- 2 tbsp flaxseed meal
- 1 tbsp peanut butter (unsalted, xylitol-free)

Prep. time: 15 min	Cook time: 0 min

DIRECTIONS

1. Combine the chopped chicken, spinach, rolled oats, pumpkin puree, flaxseed meal, and peanut butter in a large mixing bowl.
2. Mix until all ingredients are well incorporated.
3. Scoop small portions of the mixture and roll them into bite-sized balls.
4. Place the balls on a tray lined with parchment paper and refrigerate for at least 30 minutes until firm.

TURKEY AND CARROT SQUARES

20% protein, 35% carbohydrates, 15% fat, 12% minerals, 8% fiber, 5% cholesterol, 3% sodium, 2% potassium
Total Calories: 290 kcal (1.02 kcal/g, 29.0 kcal/oz)
Total Recipe Amount: 10 oz (283.5 g)

INGREDIENTS

- 1 cup cooked turkey breast, chopped
- 1/2 cup grated carrot
- 1/4 cup rolled oats
- 1 tbsp coconut oil

Prep. time: 15 min	Cook time: 0 min

DIRECTIONS

1. Combine the chopped turkey, grated carrot, rolled oats, and coconut oil in a large mixing bowl.
2. Mix until well combined.
3. Press the mixture into a greased baking dish and refrigerate for at least 1 hour before cutting into squares and serving.

TURKEY AND SWEET POTATO BALLS

26% protein, 30% carbohydrates, 10% fat, 7% minerals, 6% fiber, 4% cholesterol, 5% sodium, 7% potassium
Total Calories: 340 kcal (1.20 kcal/g, 34.0 kcal/oz)
Total Recipe Amount: 10 oz (283.5 g)

INGREDIENTS

- 1 cup cooked turkey, finely chopped
- 1/2 cup mashed sweet potato
- 1/4 cup rolled oats
- 2 tbsp peanut butter (unsalted, xylitol-free)
- 1 tbsp honey

Prep. time: 15 min   Cook time: 0 min

DIRECTIONS

1. Combine all ingredients and mix well in a large bowl.
2. Form the mixture into small, bite-sized balls.
3. Place the balls on a parchment-lined baking sheet.
4. Refrigerate for at least 30 minutes to set.

TURKEY AND BLUEBERRY TREATS

22% protein, 38% carbohydrates, 10% fat, 8% minerals, 7% fiber, 5% cholesterol, 5% sodium, 5% potassium
Total Calories: 330 kcal (1.16 kcal/g, 33.0 kcal/oz)
Total Recipe Amount: 10 oz (283.5 g)

INGREDIENTS

- 1 cup cooked turkey, shredded
- 1/2 cup fresh blueberries
- 1/4 cup rolled oats
- 2 tbsp pumpkin puree
- 1 tbsp flaxseed meal

Prep. time: 15 min   Cook time: 0 min

DIRECTIONS

1. Combine shredded turkey, fresh blueberries, rolled oats, pumpkin puree, and flaxseed meal in a large bowl.
2. Mix well until all ingredients are evenly combined.
3. Form the mixture into small bite-sized balls.
4. Refrigerate for at least 1 hour before serving.

DUCK AND APPLE BITES

30% protein, 30% carbohydrates, 15% fat, 10% minerals, 6% fiber, 5% cholesterol, 2% sodium, 2% potassium
Total Calories: 350 kcal (1.24 kcal/g, 35.1 kcal/oz)
Total Recipe Amount: 10 oz (283.5 g)

INGREDIENTS

- 1 cup cooked duck, shredded
- 1/2 cup finely chopped apples
- 1/4 cup rolled oats
- 2 tbsp plain Greek yogurt
- 1 tbsp chia seeds

Prep. time: 15 min   Cook time: 0 min

DIRECTIONS

1. Combine shredded duck, chopped apples, rolled oats, plain Greek yogurt, and chia seeds in a large bowl.
2. Mix well until all ingredients are evenly combined.
3. Form the mixture into small bite-sized balls.
4. Refrigerate for at least 1 hour before serving.

DUCK AND SWEET POTATO BALLS

24% protein, 35% carbohydrates, 15% fat, 10% minerals, 5% fiber, 5% cholesterol, 3% sodium, 3% potassium
Total Calories: 400 kcal (1.27 kcal/g, 36.1 kcal/oz)
Total Recipe Amount: 11.08 oz (314 g)

INGREDIENTS

- 1 cup shredded duck meat
- 1/2 cup mashed sweet potato
- 1/2 cup rolled oats
- 1/4 cup plain Greek yogurt
- 1 tbsp chia seeds

Prep. time: 15 min   Cook time: 0 min

DIRECTIONS

1. Combine shredded duck meat, mashed sweet potato, rolled oats, Greek yogurt, and chia seeds in a large bowl.
2. Mix thoroughly until all ingredients are well combined.
3. Form the mixture into small, bite-sized balls.
4. Refrigerate for at least 30 minutes before serving.

DUCK AND BERRY DELIGHT

30% protein, 30% carbohydrates, 15% fat, 10% minerals, 6% fiber, 5% cholesterol, 2% sodium, 2% potassium
Total Calories: 350 kcal (1.24 kcal/g, 35.1 kcal/oz)
Total Recipe Amount: 10 oz (283.5 g)

INGREDIENTS

- 1 cup ground duck
- 1/2 cup blueberries
- 1/2 cup cranberries
- 1/4 cup rolled oats
- 1 tbsp flaxseed oil
- 1/4 cup finely chopped spinach

Prep. time: 20 min   Cook time: 0 min

DIRECTIONS

1. Mix the ground duck, blueberries, cranberries, rolled oats, flaxseed oil, and finely chopped spinach in a large bowl.
2. Stir the mixture until all ingredients are evenly distributed.
3. Roll the mixture into bite-sized balls.
4. Refrigerate for at least 30 minutes before serving

BEEF AND CARROT BITES

28% protein, 32% carbohydrates, 12% fat, 7% minerals, 8% fiber, 3% cholesterol, 5% sodium, 5% potassium
Total Calories: 310 kcal (1.10 kcal/g, 31.2 kcal/oz)
Total Recipe Amount: 10 oz (283.5 g)

INGREDIENTS

- 2 cups finely grated carrots
- 1 cup ground beef
- 1 cup rolled oats
  - 1/2 cup peanut butter (unsalted, xylitol-free)
- 1/4 cup finely chopped parsley

Prep. time: 15 min   Cook time: 0 min

DIRECTIONS

1. Combine the grated carrots, ground beef, rolled oats, peanut butter, and parsley in a large bowl. Mix well until all ingredients are thoroughly combined.
2. Roll the mixture into small bite-sized balls about 1 inch in diameter.
3. Place the balls on a parchment-lined baking sheet and refrigerate for 1 hour to firm up.
4. Store the bites in an airtight container in the refrigerator for up to a week.

RAW VEGGIE AND BEEF MIX

25% protein, 35% carbohydrates, 10% fat, 8% minerals, 7% fiber, 5% cholesterol, 5% sodium, 5% potassium
Total Calories: 340 kcal (1.20 kcal/g, 34.0 kcal/oz)
Total Recipe Amount: 10 oz (283.5 g)

INGREDIENTS

- 1 cup ground beef
- 1 cup shredded carrots
- 1 cup chopped spinach
- 1/2 cup diced apples (remove seeds and core)
- 1/4 cup chopped parsley

Prep. time: 10 min   Cook time: 0 min

DIRECTIONS

1. Combine ground beef, shredded carrots, chopped spinach, diced apples, and chopped parsley in a large bowl.
2. Mix all ingredients thoroughly until they are evenly distributed.
3. Serve immediately or store in the refrigerator for up to 3 days.

PORK AND APPLE BITES

25% protein, 30% carbohydrates, 15% fat, 10% minerals, 8% fiber, 5% cholesterol, 5% sodium, 2% potassium
Total Calories: 360 kcal (1.27 kcal/g, 36.1 kcal/oz)
Total Recipe Amount: 10 oz (283.5 g)

INGREDIENTS

- 1 cup ground pork
- 1/2 cup finely chopped apples
- 1/4 cup rolled oats
- 1 tbsp honey
- 1 tsp cinnamon

Prep. time: 10 min   Cook time: 0 min

DIRECTIONS

1. Mix ground pork, chopped apples, rolled oats, honey, and cinnamon in a large bowl.
2. Form the mixture into small bite-sized balls.
3. Refrigerate for at least 1 hour before serving.

PORK AND PINEAPPLE ROLLS

22% protein, 38% carbohydrates, 10% fat, 8% minerals, 7% fiber, 5% cholesterol, 5% sodium, 5% potassium
Total Calories: 330 kcal (1.16 kcal/g, 33.0 kcal/oz)
Total Recipe Amount: 10 oz (283.5 g)

INGREDIENTS

- 1 cup ground pork
- 1/2 cup finely chopped pineapple
- 1/4 cup quinoa, cooked
- 1 tbsp parsley, chopped
- 1 tsp olive oil

Prep. time: 15 min	Cook time: 0 min

DIRECTIONS

1. Combine ground pork, chopped pineapple, cooked quinoa, parsley, and olive oil in a large bowl.
2. Roll the mixture into small rolls.
3. Refrigerate for at least 1 hour before serving.

PORK AND SPINACH TREATS

28% protein, 32% carbohydrates, 12% fat, 7% minerals, 8% fiber, 3% cholesterol, 5% sodium, 5% potassium
Total Calories: 310 kcal (1.10 kcal/g, 31.2 kcal/oz)
Total Recipe Amount: 10 oz (283.5 g)

INGREDIENTS

- 1 cup ground pork
- 1/2 cup finely chopped apples
- 1/4 cup rolled oats
- 1 tbsp honey
- 1 tsp cinnamon

Prep. time: 10 min	Cook time: 0 min

DIRECTIONS

1. Mix ground pork, chopped spinach, cooked brown rice, flaxseed meal, and turmeric in a large bowl.
2. Form the mixture into small, treat-sized shapes.
3. Refrigerate for at least 1 hour before serving.

WHITE FISH AND SWEET POTATO MEDLEY

35% protein, 40% carbohydrates, 15% fat, 5% minerals, 3% fiber, 2% cholesterol, 0.5% sodium, 1.5% potassium
Total Calories: 600 kcal (1.01 kcal/g, 28.6 kcal/oz)
Total Recipe Amount: 21 oz (600 g)

INGREDIENTS

- 1 1/2 cups boneless, skinless white fish, chopped
- 2 medium sweet potatoes, peeled and diced
- 1 tbsp olive oil
- 1 cup of green beans, chopped
- 1/4 tsp turmeric powder
- 1/4 tsp dried parsley

Prep. time: 15 min   Cook time: 30 min

DIRECTIONS

1. Bring water to a boil in a large pot and add the diced sweet potatoes. Cook for 10-15 minutes until tender. Drain and set aside.
2. In a large skillet, heat the olive oil over medium heat. Add the chopped fish and cook for about 5-7 minutes, until fully cooked and flaky.
3. Add the green beans to the skillet with the fish and cook for 5 minutes. Stir in the cooked sweet potatoes, turmeric powder, and dried parsley. Mix well and cook for 3-5 minutes to ensure everything is heated.
4. Allow the medley to cool before serving it to your dog.

WHITE FISH AND KALE ROLLS

35% protein, 25% carbohydrates, 20% fat, 8% minerals, 5% fiber, 2% cholesterol, 3% sodium, 2% potassium
Total Calories: 350 kcal (1.20 kcal/g, 35 kcal/oz)
Total Recipe Amount: 10 oz (283.5 g)

INGREDIENTS

- 1 cup cooked white fish, finely chopped
- 1 cup fresh kale, finely chopped
- 1/4 cup rolled oats
- 1 tbsp flaxseed meal
- 1 tbsp olive oil

Prep. time: 20 min   Cook time: 0 min

DIRECTIONS

1. Combine the chopped white fish, chopped kale, rolled oats, and flaxseed meal in a large bowl. Mix well.
2. Shape the mixture into small, cylindrical rolls.
3. Place the rolls on a tray and refrigerate for at least 30 minutes before serving.

LIVER AND PUMPKIN BITES

30% protein, 30% carbohydrates, 25% fat, 8% minerals, 5% fiber, 1% cholesterol, 0.5% sodium, 0.5% potassium
Total Calories: 300 kcal (1.06 kcal/g, 30.0 kcal/oz)
Total Recipe Amount: 10 oz (283.5 g)

INGREDIENTS

- 1 cup cooked liver, chopped
- 1/2 cup canned pumpkin (not pumpkin pie filling)
- 1/3 cup rolled oats
- 1 tbsp flaxseed meal
- 1 tbsp olive oil

Prep. time: 20 min   Cook time: 0 min

DIRECTIONS

1. Combine the chopped liver, canned pumpkin, rolled oats, and flaxseed meal in a large bowl. Mix well.
2. Shape the mixture into small, bite-sized balls.
3. Place the bites on a tray and refrigerate for at least 30 minutes before serving.

LIVER AND BARLEY SOUP

25% protein, 40% carbohydrates, 20% fat, 10% minerals, 4% fiber, 0.5% cholesterol, 0.5% sodium, 0.5% potassium
Total Calories: 200 kcal (0.58 kcal/g, 16.6 kcal/oz)
Total Recipe Amount: 12 oz (340 g)

INGREDIENTS

- 1 cup cooked liver, chopped
- 3/4 cup cooked barley
- 1/2 cup carrots, diced
- 1 cup low-sodium chicken broth

Prep. time: 10 min   Cook time: 20 min

DIRECTIONS

1. Combine the chopped liver, cooked barley, diced carrots, and chicken broth in a pot.
2. Bring to a boil, then reduce heat and simmer for 20 minutes.

HEART AND BROCCOLI STIR-FRY

28% protein, 30% carbohydrates, 20% fat, 10% minerals, 6% fiber, 3% cholesterol, 2% sodium, 1% potassium
Total Calories: 300 kcal (1.06 kcal/g, 30.0 kcal/oz)
Total Recipe Amount: 10 oz (283.5 g)

INGREDIENTS

- 1 cup cooked heart, chopped
- 1 cup broccoli florets
- 1/2 cup carrots, julienned
- 1 tbsp olive oil
- 1/4 cup low-sodium chicken broth

Prep. time: 15 min   Cook time: 20 min

DIRECTIONS

1. Heat olive oil in a large skillet over medium heat.
2. Add the chopped heart and cook for 5-7 minutes, stirring occasionally.
3. Add the broccoli and carrots to the skillet, and pour in the chicken broth. Cook for 10-12 minutes until the vegetables are tender and the heart is fully cooked.
4. Allow to cool before serving.

LIVER AND SWEET CORN FRITTERS

30% protein, 28% carbohydrates, 20% fat, 7% minerals, 5% fiber, 4% cholesterol, 3% sodium, 3% potassium
Total Calories: 350 kcal (1.23 kcal/g, 35.0 kcal/oz)
Total Recipe Amount: 10 oz (283.5 g)

INGREDIENTS

- 1 cup cooked liver, chopped
- 1 cup sweet corn kernels
- 1 egg
- 1/2 cup whole wheat flour
- 1 tbsp olive oil

Prep. time: 10 min   Cook time: 20 min

DIRECTIONS

1. Combine the chopped liver, sweet corn, and egg in a mixing bowl. Mix until well combined.
2. Gradually add the whole wheat flour to the mixture until it becomes batter-like.
3. Heat olive oil in a large skillet over medium heat. Drop spoonfuls of the mixture into the skillet, flattening slightly to form fritters.
4. Cook for 3-4 minutes on each side, until golden brown and cooked through. Allow to cool before serving.

HEART AND SWEET POTATO BALLS

32% protein, 28% carbohydrates, 25% fat, 8% minerals, 5% fiber, 1% cholesterol, 0.5% sodium, 0.5% potassium
Total Calories: 320 kcal (1.02 kcal/g, 29.0 kcal/oz)
Total Recipe Amount: 11 oz (312 g)

INGREDIENTS

- 1 cup cooked beef heart, finely chopped
- 1/2 cup cooked sweet potato, mashed
- 2/3 cup rolled oats
- 1 tbsp flaxseed meal
- 1 tbsp olive oil

Prep. time: 20 min   Cook time: 0 min

DIRECTIONS

1. Combine the chopped beef heart, mashed sweet potato, rolled oats, and flaxseed meal in a large bowl. Mix well.
2. Shape the mixture into small balls.
3. Place the balls on a tray and refrigerate for at least 30 minutes before serving.

KIDNEY AND CARROT TREATS

30% protein, 30% carbohydrates, 25% fat, 8% minerals, 5% fiber, 1% cholesterol, 0.5% sodium, 0.5% potassium
Total Calories: 300 kcal (1.05 kcal/g, 30.0 kcal/oz)
Total Recipe Amount: 10 oz (285 g)

INGREDIENTS

- 1 cup cooked kidney, finely chopped
- 1 cup grated carrots
- 1/3 cup rolled oats
- 1 tbsp flaxseed meal
- 1 tbsp olive oil

Prep. time: 20 min   Cook time: 0 min

DIRECTIONS

1. Combine the chopped kidney, grated carrots, rolled oats, and flaxseed meal in a large bowl. Mix well.
2. Shape the mixture into small, bite-sized balls.
3. Place the treats on a tray and refrigerate for at least 30 minutes before serving.

RABBIT AND APPLE BITES

35% protein, 25% carbohydrates, 20% fat, 10% minerals, 5% fiber, 1% cholesterol, 0.5% sodium, 0.5% potassium
Total Calories: 350 kcal (1.22 kcal/g, 35.0 kcal/oz)
Total Recipe Amount: 10 oz (285 g)

INGREDIENTS

- 1 cup cooked rabbit, finely chopped
- 1/2 cup grated apple
- 1/3 cup rolled oats
- 1 tbsp flaxseed meal
- 1 tbsp olive oil

Prep. time: 20 min   Cook time: 0 min

DIRECTIONS

1. Combine the chopped rabbit, grated apple, rolled oats, and flaxseed meal in a large bowl. Mix well.
2. Shape the mixture into small, bite-sized balls.
3. Place the bites on a tray and refrigerate for at least 30 minutes before serving.

RABBIT AND SWEET POTATO BALLS

32% protein, 28% carbohydrates, 25% fat, 8% minerals, 5% fiber, 1% cholesterol, 0.5% sodium, 0.5% potassium
Total Calories: 320 kcal (1.12 kcal/g, 32.0 kcal/oz)
Total Recipe Amount: 10 oz (285 g)

INGREDIENTS

- 1 cup cooked rabbit, finely chopped
- 1/2 cup cooked sweet potato, mashed
- 2/3 cup rolled oats
- 1 tbsp flaxseed meal
- 1 tbsp olive oil

Prep. time: 20 min   Cook time: 0 min

DIRECTIONS

1. Combine the chopped rabbit, mashed sweet potato, rolled oats, and flaxseed meal in a large bowl. Mix well.
2. Shape the mixture into small balls.
3. Place the balls on a tray and refrigerate for at least 30 minutes before serving.

RABBIT AND SPINACH WRAPS

35% protein, 20% carbohydrates, 25% fat, 10% minerals, 5% fiber, 1% cholesterol, 0.5% sodium, 0.5% potassium
Total Calories: 350 kcal (1.23 kcal/g, 35.0 kcal/oz)
Total Recipe Amount: 10 oz (285 g)

INGREDIENTS

- 1 cup cooked rabbit, finely chopped
- 1/2 cup fresh spinach, finely chopped
- 1/3 cup rolled oats
- 1 tbsp flaxseed meal
- 1 tbsp olive oil

Prep. time: 20 min   Cook time: 0 min

DIRECTIONS

1. Combine the chopped rabbit, chopped spinach, rolled oats, and flaxseed meal in a large bowl. Mix well.
2. Shape the mixture into small, cylindrical wraps.
3. Place the wraps on a tray and refrigerate for at least 30 minutes before serving.

LAMB AND APPLE SQUARES

22% protein, 34% carbohydrates, 12% fat, 10% minerals, 8% fiber, 5% cholesterol, 4% sodium, 3% potassium
Total Calories: 320 kcal (1.13 kcal/g, 32.0 kcal/oz)
Total Recipe Amount: 10 oz (283.5 g)

INGREDIENTS

- 1 cup cooked lamb, chopped
- 1/2 cup grated apple
- 1/4 cup rolled oats
- 1 tbsp honey

Prep. time: 15 min   Cook time: 0 min

DIRECTIONS

1. Combine the chopped lamb, grated apple, rolled oats, and honey in a large mixing bowl.
2. Mix until well combined.
3. Press the mixture into a greased baking dish and refrigerate for at least 1 hour before cutting into squares and serving.

LAMB AND PEAR BALLS

30% protein, 30% carbohydrates, 25% fat, 8% minerals, 5% fiber, 1% cholesterol, 0.5% sodium, 0.5% potassium
Total Calories: 300 kcal (1.05 kcal/g, 30.0 kcal/oz)
Total Recipe Amount: 10 oz (285 g)

INGREDIENTS

- 1 cup cooked lamb, finely chopped
- 1/2 cup grated pear
- 1/3 cup rolled oats
- 1 tbsp flaxseed meal
- 1 tbsp olive oil

Prep. time: 20 min   **Cook time: 0 min**

DIRECTIONS

1. Combine the chopped lamb, grated pear, rolled oats, and flaxseed meal in a large bowl. Mix well.
2. Shape the mixture into small balls.
3. Place the balls on a tray and refrigerate for at least 30 minutes before serving.

LAMB AND KALE BOWL

35% protein, 25% carbohydrates, 25% fat, 8% minerals, 5% fiber, 1% cholesterol, 0.5% sodium, 0.5% potassium
Total Calories: 350 kcal (1.23 kcal/g, 35.0 kcal/oz)
Total Recipe Amount: 10 oz (285 g)

INGREDIENTS

- 1 cup cooked lamb, finely chopped
- 4 cups fresh kale, finely chopped
- 1/3 cup rolled oats
- 1 tbsp flaxseed meal
- 1 tbsp olive oil

Prep. time: 20 min   **Cook time: 0 min**

DIRECTIONS

1. Combine the chopped lamb, chopped kale, rolled oats, and flaxseed meal in a large bowl. Mix well.
2. Shape the mixture into a bowl-like shape.
3. Place the bowl on a tray and refrigerate for at least 30 minutes before serving.

VENISON AND CUCUMBER FRESH DISH

30% protein, 30% carbohydrates, 25% fat, 8% minerals, 5% fiber, 1% cholesterol, 0.5% sodium, 0.5% potassium
Total Calories: 300 kcal (1.05 kcal/g, 30.0 kcal/oz)
Total Recipe Amount: 10 oz (285 g)

INGREDIENTS

- 1 cup cooked venison, finely chopped
- 1/2 cup diced cucumber
- 1/3 cup rolled oats
- 1 tbsp flaxseed meal
- 1 tbsp olive oil

Prep. time: 20 min   Cook time: 0 min

DIRECTIONS

1. Combine the chopped venison, diced cucumber, rolled oats, and flaxseed meal in a large bowl. Mix well.
2. Shape the mixture into a dish-like shape.
3. Place the dish on a tray and refrigerate for at least 30 minutes before serving.

VENISON AND SWEET POTATO SALAD

32% protein, 28% carbohydrates, 25% fat, 8% minerals, 5% fiber, 1% cholesterol, 0.5% sodium, 0.5% potassium
Total Calories: 320 kcal (0.94 kcal/g, 26.6 kcal/oz)
Total Recipe Amount: 12 oz (340 g)

INGREDIENTS

- 1 cup cooked venison, finely chopped
- 1/2 cup cooked sweet potato, diced
- 2/3 cup rolled oats
- 1 tbsp flaxseed meal
- 1 tbsp olive oil

Prep. time: 20 min   Cook time: 0 min

DIRECTIONS

1. Combine the chopped venison, diced sweet potato, rolled oats, and flaxseed meal in a large bowl. Mix well.
2. Shape the mixture into a salad-like shape.
3. Place the salad on a tray and refrigerate for at least 30 minutes before serving.

RAW VENISON AND CARROT MIX

35% protein, 25% carbohydrates, 25% fat, 8% minerals, 5% fiber, 1% cholesterol, 0.5% sodium, 0.5% potassium
Total Calories: 350 kcal (1.23 kcal/g, 35.0 kcal/oz)
Total Recipe Amount: 10 oz (285 g)

INGREDIENTS

- 1 cup raw venison, finely chopped
- 1 cup grated carrots
- 1/3 cup rolled oats
- 1 tbsp flaxseed meal
- 1 tbsp olive oil

Prep. time: 20 min   Cook time: 0 min

DIRECTIONS

1. Combine the chopped raw venison, grated carrots, rolled oats, and flaxseed meal in a large bowl. Mix well.
2. Shape the mixture into a mix-like shape.
3. Place the mix on a tray and refrigerate for at least 30 minutes before serving.

PEANUT BUTTER AND OAT BALLS

20% protein, 40% carbohydrates, 30% fat, 5% minerals, 3% fiber, 1% cholesterol, 0.5% sodium, 0.5% potassium
Total Calories: 400 kcal (1.40 kcal/g, 40.0 kcal/oz)
Total Recipe Amount: 10 oz (285 g)

INGREDIENTS

- 1/2 cup peanut butter (unsalted, xylitol-free)
- 1 1/3 cups rolled oats
- 1/8 cup honey
- 1/3 cup flaxseed meal

Prep. time: 20 min   Cook time: 0 min

DIRECTIONS

1. Combine the peanut butter, rolled oats, honey, and flaxseed meal in a large bowl. Mix well.
2. Shape the mixture into small balls.
3. Place the balls on a tray and refrigerate for at least 30 minutes before serving.

PUMPKIN AND CARROT TREATS

20% protein, 40% carbohydrates, 30% fat, 5% minerals, 3% fiber, 1% cholesterol, 0.5% sodium, 0.5% potassium
Total Calories: 400 kcal (1.40 kcal/g, 40.0 kcal/oz)
Total Recipe Amount: 10 oz (285 g)

INGREDIENTS

| Prep. time: 20 min | Cook time: 0 min |

- 1/2 cup canned pumpkin (not pumpkin pie filling)
- 1 cup grated carrots
- 1/3 cup rolled oats
- 1/3 cup flaxseed meal

DIRECTIONS

1. Combine the canned pumpkin, grated carrots, rolled oats, and flaxseed meal in a large bowl. Mix well.
2. Shape the mixture into small, bite-sized balls.
3. Place the treats on a tray and refrigerate for at least 30 minutes before serving.

YOGURT AND BERRY PARFAIT

25% protein, 40% carbohydrates, 20% fat, 10% minerals, 3% fiber, 1% cholesterol, 0.5% sodium, 0.5% potassium
Total Calories: 250 kcal (0.87 kcal/g, 25.0 kcal/oz)
Total Recipe Amount: 10 oz (285 g)

INGREDIENTS

| Prep. time: 10 min | Cook time: 0 min |

- 3/4 cup plain Greek yogurt
- 1/2 cup mixed berries (blueberries, strawberries, raspberries)
- 1/3 cup rolled oats

DIRECTIONS

1. Layer the Greek yogurt, mixed berries, and rolled oats in a large bowl.
2. Repeat the layers until all ingredients are used.
3. Serve immediately or refrigerate for up to 30 minutes before serving.

SLOW-COOKED

CHICKEN AND BROWN RICE STEW

28% protein, 32% carbohydrates, 18% fat, 6% minerals, 8% fiber, 2% cholesterol, 3% sodium, 3% potassium
Total Calories: 700 kcal (0.78 kcal/g, 22.05 kcal/oz)
Total Recipe Amount: 31.75 oz (900 g)

INGREDIENTS

- 1 cup cooked chicken breast, chopped
- 1/2 cup brown rice, uncooked
- 1 cup chopped green beans
- 1 cup carrots, diced
- 1/2 cup peas
- 3 cups low-sodium chicken broth

Prep. time: 15 min   Cook time: 240 min

DIRECTIONS

1. Combine all ingredients in a slow cooker.
2. Cook on low for 4 hours or until the rice is tender and the chicken is fully cooked.
3. Allow to cool before serving.

CHICKEN AND SWEET POTATO CASSEROLE

30% protein, 30% carbohydrates, 20% fat, 7% minerals, 7% fiber, 2% cholesterol, 2% sodium, 2% potassium
Total Calories: 780 kcal (1.13 kcal/g, 32 kcal/oz)
Total Recipe Amount: 24.4 oz (690 g)

INGREDIENTS

- 2 cups cooked, shredded chicken
- 1 cup chopped sweet potato
- 1 cup chopped carrots
- 1/2 cup peas
- 1 cup cooked quinoa
- 2 cups low-sodium chicken broth

Prep. time: 15 min   Cook time: 240 min

DIRECTIONS

1. Combine all ingredients in a slow cooker.
2. Cook on low for 4 hours or until the sweet potatoes are tender and the chicken is fully cooked.
3. Allow to cool before serving.

CHICKEN AND CARROT SOUP

25% protein, 35% carbohydrates, 15% fat, 10% minerals, 7% fiber, 2% cholesterol, 3% sodium, 3% potassium
Total Calories: 600 kcal (0.95 kcal/g, 27 kcal/oz)
Total Recipe Amount: 22.2 oz (630 g)

INGREDIENTS

- 2 cups cooked, shredded chicken
- 2 cups chopped carrots
- 1 cup chopped celery
- 1/2 cup peas
- 3 cups low-sodium chicken broth

Prep. time: 15 min   Cook time: 240 min

DIRECTIONS

1. Combine all ingredients in a slow cooker.
2. Cook on low for 4 hours or until the carrots and celery are tender and the chicken is fully cooked.
3. Allow to cool before serving.

TURKEY AND QUINOA STEW

30% protein, 30% carbohydrates, 20% fat, 8% minerals, 6% fiber, 3% cholesterol, 2% sodium, 1% potassium
Total Calories: 750 kcal (1.02 kcal/g, 28.93 kcal/oz)
Total Recipe Amount: 26 oz (737 g)

INGREDIENTS

- 2 cups cooked, shredded turkey
- 1 cup cooked quinoa
- 1 cup chopped carrots
- 1 cup chopped spinach
- 1/2 cup peas
- 2 cups low-sodium turkey broth

Prep. time: 15 min   Cook time: 240 min

DIRECTIONS

1. Combine all ingredients in a slow cooker.
2. Cook on low for 4 hours or until the quinoa is tender and the turkey is fully cooked.
3. Allow to cool before serving.

TURKEY AND PUMPKIN CASSEROLE

28% protein, 32% carbohydrates, 18% fat, 8% minerals, 6% fiber, 2% cholesterol, 3% sodium, 3% potassium
Total Calories: 820 kcal (1.07 kcal/g, 30.4 kcal/oz)
Total Recipe Amount: 27 oz (770 g)

INGREDIENTS

- 2 cups cooked, shredded turkey
- 1 cup pumpkin puree
- 1 cup chopped carrots
- 1 cup cooked quinoa
- 1/2 cup peas
- 2 cups low-sodium turkey broth

Prep. time: 15 min   Cook time: 240 min

DIRECTIONS

1. Combine all ingredients in a slow cooker.
2. Cook on low for 4 hours or until the quinoa is tender and the turkey is fully cooked.
3. Allow to cool before serving.

TURKEY AND SPINACH SOUP

30% protein, 30% carbohydrates, 20% fat, 8% minerals, 6% fiber, 2% cholesterol, 2% sodium, 2% potassium
Total Calories: 780 kcal (0.97 kcal/g, 27.5 kcal/oz)
Total Recipe Amount: 28.4 oz (800 g)

INGREDIENTS

- 2 cups cooked, shredded turkey
- 2 cups chopped spinach
- 1 cup chopped carrots
- 1/2 cup peas
- 1/2 cup quinoa
- 3 cups low-sodium turkey broth

Prep. time: 10 min   Cook time: 240 min

DIRECTIONS

1. Combine all ingredients in a slow cooker.
2. Cook on low for 4 hours or until the spinach is wilted and the turkey is fully cooked.
3. Allow to cool before serving.

DUCK AND QUINOA RAGOUT

32% protein, 28% carbohydrates, 25% fat, 7% minerals, 5% fiber, 2% cholesterol, 1% sodium, 0.5% potassium
Total Calories: 920 kcal (1.23 kcal/g, 34.8 kcal/oz)
Total Recipe Amount: 26.4 oz (750 g)

INGREDIENTS

- 2 cups cooked, shredded duck
- 1 cup cooked quinoa
- 1 cup chopped carrots
- 1 cup chopped spinach
- 1/2 cup peas
- 2 cups low-sodium duck broth

Prep. time: 15 min   Cook time: 240 min

DIRECTIONS

1. Combine all ingredients in a slow cooker.
2. Cook on low for 4 hours or until the quinoa is tender and the duck is fully cooked.
3. Allow to cool before serving.

DUCK AND CARROT CASSEROLE

30% protein, 30% carbohydrates, 20% fat, 10% minerals, 5% fiber, 2% cholesterol, 2% sodium, 1% potassium
Total Calories: 870 kcal (1.15 kcal/g, 32.66 kcal/oz)
Total Recipe Amount: 26.6 oz (770 g)

INGREDIENTS

- 2 cups cooked, shredded duck
- 2 cups chopped carrots
- 1 cup cooked brown rice
- 1/2 cup peas
- 2 cups low-sodium duck broth

Prep. time: 15 min   Cook time: 240 min

DIRECTIONS

1. Combine all ingredients in a slow cooker.
2. Cook on low for 4 hours until the rice and carrots are tender and the duck is fully cooked.
3. Allow to cool before serving.

DUCK AND VEGETABLE MEDLEY

28% protein, 32% carbohydrates, 18% fat, 8% minerals, 7% fiber, 3% cholesterol, 2% sodium, 2% potassium
Total Calories: 850 kcal (1.12 kcal/g, 31.8 kcal/oz)
Total Recipe Amount: 26.7 oz (760 g)

INGREDIENTS

- 2 cups cooked, shredded duck
- 1 cup chopped carrots
- 1 cup chopped green beans
- 1 cup chopped sweet potatoes
- 1/2 cup peas
- 2 cups low-sodium duck broth

Prep. time: 15 min   Cook time: 240 min

DIRECTIONS

1. Combine all ingredients in a slow cooker.
2. Cook on low for 4 hours or until the vegetables are tender and the duck is fully cooked.
3. Allow to cool before serving.

BEEF AND BARLEY STEW

30% protein, 30% carbohydrates, 20% fat, 10% minerals, 5% fiber, 2% cholesterol, 2% sodium, 1% potassium
Total Calories: 800 kcal (1.04 kcal/g, 29.5 kcal/oz)
Total Recipe Amount: 27.1 oz (765 g)

INGREDIENTS

- 2 cups cooked, shredded beef
- 1 cup chopped carrots
- 1 cup chopped green beans
- 1 cup cooked barley
- 1/2 cup peas
- 2 cups low-sodium beef broth

Prep. time: 15 min   Cook time: 240 min

DIRECTIONS

1. Combine all ingredients in a slow cooker.
2. Cook on low for 4 hours or until the barley is tender and the beef is fully cooked.
3. Allow to cool before serving.

BEEF AND SWEET POTATO CASSEROLE

32% protein, 28% carbohydrates, 25% fat, 7% minerals, 5% fiber, 2% cholesterol, 1% sodium, 0.5% potassium
Total Calories: 900 kcal (1.18 kcal/g, 33.5 kcal/oz)
Total Recipe Amount: 26.8 oz (760 g)

INGREDIENTS

- 2 cups cooked, shredded beef
- 2 cups chopped sweet potatoes
- 1 cup chopped carrots
- 1 cup chopped green beans
- 1/2 cup peas
- 2 cups low-sodium beef broth

Prep. time: 15 min   Cook time: 240 min

DIRECTIONS

1. Combine all ingredients in a slow cooker.
2. Cook on low for 4 hours or until the sweet potatoes are tender and the beef is fully cooked.
3. Allow to cool before serving.

BEEF AND BLUEBERRY POT

28% protein, 32% carbohydrates, 18% fat, 10% minerals, 6% fiber, 2% cholesterol, 2% sodium, 2% potassium
Total Calories: 850 kcal (1.12 kcal/g, 31.8 kcal/oz)
Total Recipe Amount: 26.8 oz (760 g)

INGREDIENTS

- 2 cups cooked, shredded beef
- 1 cup chopped carrots
- 1 cup chopped sweet potatoes
- 1/2 cup peas
- 1 cup blueberries
- 2 cups low-sodium beef broth

Prep. time: 15 min   Cook time: 240 min

DIRECTIONS

1. Combine all ingredients in a slow cooker.
2. Cook on low for 4 hours or until the sweet potatoes are tender and the beef is fully cooked.
3. Allow to cool before serving.

PORK AND BROWN RICE STEW

28% protein, 32% carbohydrates, 18% fat, 8% minerals, 7% fiber, 3% cholesterol, 2% sodium, 2% potassium
Total Calories: 850 kcal (1.11 kcal/g, 31.4 kcal/oz)
Total Recipe Amount: 27 oz (765 g)

INGREDIENTS

- 2 cups cooked, shredded pork
- 1 cup cooked brown rice
- 1 cup chopped carrots
- 1 cup chopped green beans
- 1/2 cup peas
- 2 cups low-sodium pork broth

Prep. time: 15 min	Cook time: 240 min

DIRECTIONS

1. Combine all ingredients in a slow cooker.
2. Cook on low for 4 hours or until the rice is tender and the pork is fully cooked.
3. Allow to cool before serving.

PORK AND SWEET POTATO CHOWDER

30% protein, 30% carbohydrates, 20% fat, 10% minerals, 5% fiber, 2% cholesterol, 2% sodium, 1% potassium
Total Calories: 900 kcal (1.18 kcal/g, 33.5 kcal/oz)
Total Recipe Amount: 26.8 oz (760 g)

INGREDIENTS

- 2 cups cooked, shredded pork
- 2 cups chopped sweet potatoes
- 1 cup chopped carrots
- 1 cup chopped green beans
- 1/2 cup peas
- 2 cups low-sodium pork broth

Prep. time: 15 min	Cook time: 240 min

DIRECTIONS

1. Combine all ingredients in a slow cooker.
2. Cook on low for 4 hours or until the sweet potatoes are tender and the pork is fully cooked.
3. Allow to cool before serving.

SALMON AND BROCCOLI STEW

30% protein, 30% carbohydrates, 20% fat, 10% minerals, 5% fiber, 2% cholesterol, 2% sodium, 1% potassium
Total Calories: 820 kcal (1.07 kcal/g, 30.36 kcal/oz)
Total Recipe Amount: 27 oz (765 g)

INGREDIENTS

- 2 cups cooked, flaked salmon
- 2 cups chopped broccoli
- 1 cup chopped carrots
- 1 cup chopped sweet potatoes
- 1/2 cup peas
- 2 cups low-sodium vegetable broth

Prep. time: 15 min   Cook time: 240 min

DIRECTIONS

1. Combine all ingredients in a slow cooker.
2. Cook on low for 4 hours or until the sweet potatoes are tender and the salmon is fully cooked.
3. Allow to cool before serving.

WHITE FISH AND SWEET CORN CHOWDER

28% protein, 32% carbohydrates, 18% fat, 10% minerals, 7% fiber, 3% cholesterol, 2% sodium, 2% potassium
Total Calories: 810 kcal (1.06 kcal/g, 30.08 kcal/oz)
Total Recipe Amount: 27 oz (765 g)

INGREDIENTS

- 2 cups cooked, flaked white fish
- 2 cups sweet corn
- 1 cup chopped carrots
- 1 cup chopped sweet potatoes
- 1/2 cup peas
- 2 cups low-sodium fish broth

Prep. time: 10 min   Cook time: 240 min

DIRECTIONS

1. Combine all ingredients in a slow cooker.
2. Cook on low for 4 hours or until the sweet potatoes are tender and the fish is fully cooked.
3. Allow to cool before serving.

WHITE FISH AND LENTIL CURRY

30% protein, 30% carbohydrates, 20% fat, 10% minerals, 5% fiber, 2% cholesterol, 2% sodium, 1% potassium
Total Calories: 820 kcal (1.07 kcal/g, 30.36 kcal/oz)
Total Recipe Amount: 27 oz (765 g)

INGREDIENTS

- 2 cups cooked, flaked white fish
- 1 cup cooked lentils
- 1 cup chopped carrots
- 1 cup chopped sweet potatoes
- 1/2 cup peas
- 2 cups low-sodium vegetable broth
- 1 tsp turmeric (optional, for anti-inflammatory benefits)

Prep. time: 15 min   Cook time: 240 min

DIRECTIONS

1. Combine all ingredients in a slow cooker.
2. Cook on low for 4 hours or until the lentils are tender and the fish is fully cooked.
3. Allow to cool before serving.

LIVER AND BROWN RICE STEW

30% protein, 30% carbohydrates, 20% fat, 10% minerals, 5% fiber, 2% cholesterol, 2% sodium, 1% potassium
Total Calories: 850 kcal (1.11 kcal/g, 31.4 kcal/oz)
Total Recipe Amount: 27 oz (765 g)

INGREDIENTS

- 2 cups cooked, chopped liver
- 1 cup cooked brown rice
- 1 cup chopped carrots
- 1 cup chopped green beans
- 1/2 cup peas
- 2 cups low-sodium beef broth

Prep. time: 15 min   Cook time: 240 min

DIRECTIONS

1. Combine all ingredients in a slow cooker.
2. Cook on low for 4 hours or until the rice is tender and the liver is fully cooked.
3. Allow to cool before serving.

HEART AND SWEET POTATO CASSEROLE

30% protein, 30% carbohydrates, 20% fat, 10% minerals, 5% fiber, 2% cholesterol, 2% sodium, 1% potassium
Total Calories: 900 kcal (1.18 kcal/g, 33.5 kcal/oz)
Total Recipe Amount: 27 oz (765 g)

INGREDIENTS

- 2 cups cooked, chopped beef heart
- 2 cups chopped sweet potatoes
- 1 cup chopped carrots
- 1 cup chopped green beans
- 1/2 cup peas
- 2 cups low-sodium beef broth

Prep. time: 15 min   Cook time: 240 min

DIRECTIONS

1. Combine all ingredients in a slow cooker.
2. Cook on low for 4 hours or until the sweet potatoes are tender and the heart is fully cooked.
3. Allow to cool before serving.

KIDNEY AND VEGETABLE MEDLEY

28% protein, 32% carbohydrates, 18% fat, 10% minerals, 7% fiber, 3% cholesterol, 2% sodium, 2% potassium
Total Calories: 860 kcal (1.12 kcal/g, 31.76 kcal/oz)
Total Recipe Amount: 27 oz (765 g)

INGREDIENTS

- 2 cups cooked, chopped kidney
- 2 cups chopped carrots
- 1 cup chopped sweet potatoes
- 1 cup chopped green beans
- 1/2 cup peas
- 2 cups low-sodium beef broth

Prep. time: 10 min   Cook time: 240 min

DIRECTIONS

1. Combine all ingredients in a slow cooker.
2. Cook on low for 4 hours or until the vegetables are tender and the kidney is fully cooked.
3. Allow to cool before serving.

RABBIT AND QUINOA STEW

32% protein, 28% carbohydrates, 25% fat, 7% minerals, 5% fiber, 2% cholesterol, 1% sodium, 0.5% potassium
Total Calories: 840 kcal (1.11 kcal/g, 31.2 kcal/oz)
Total Recipe Amount: 27 oz (765 g)

INGREDIENTS

- 2 cups cooked, shredded rabbit
- 1 cup cooked quinoa
- 1 cup chopped carrots
- 1 cup chopped sweet potatoes
- 1/2 cup peas
- 2 cups low-sodium rabbit broth

Prep. time: 15 min   Cook time: 240 min

DIRECTIONS

1. Combine all ingredients in a slow cooker.
2. Cook on low for 4 hours or until the quinoa is tender and the rabbit is fully cooked.
3. Allow to cool before serving.

RABBIT AND SWEET POTATO CASSEROLE

30% protein, 30% carbohydrates, 20% fat, 10% minerals, 5% fiber, 2% cholesterol, 2% sodium, 1% potassium
Total Calories: 860 kcal (1.12 kcal/g, 31.76 kcal/oz)
Total Recipe Amount: 27 oz (765 g)

INGREDIENTS

- 2 cups cooked, shredded rabbit
- 2 cups chopped sweet potatoes
- 1 cup chopped carrots
- 1 cup chopped green beans
- 1/2 cup peas
- 2 cups low-sodium rabbit broth

Prep. time: 15 min   Cook time: 240 min

DIRECTIONS

1. Combine all ingredients in a slow cooker.
2. Cook on low for 4 hours or until the sweet potatoes are tender and the rabbit is fully cooked.
3. Allow to cool before serving.

RABBIT AND VEGETABLE MEDLEY

28% protein, 32% carbohydrates, 18% fat, 10% minerals, 7% fiber, 3% cholesterol, 2% sodium, 2% potassium
Total Calories: 840 kcal (1.11 kcal/g, 31.2 kcal/oz)
Total Recipe Amount: 27 oz (765 g)

INGREDIENTS

- 2 cups cooked, shredded rabbit
- 2 cups chopped carrots
- 1 cup chopped green beans
- 1 cup chopped sweet potatoes
- 1/2 cup peas
- 2 cups low-sodium rabbit broth

Prep. time: 10 min	Cook time: 240 min

DIRECTIONS

1. Combine all ingredients in a slow cooker.
2. Cook on low for 4 hours or until the vegetables are tender and the rabbit is fully cooked.
3. Allow to cool before serving.

LAMB AND BARLEY POT

30% protein, 30% carbohydrates, 20% fat, 10% minerals, 5% fiber, 2% cholesterol, 2% sodium, 1% potassium
Total Calories: 880 kcal (1.15 kcal/g, 32.6 kcal/oz)
Total Recipe Amount: 27 oz (765 g)

INGREDIENTS

- 2 cups cooked, shredded lamb
- 1 cup cooked barley
- 1 cup chopped carrots
- 1 cup chopped green beans
- 1/2 cup peas
- 2 cups low-sodium lamb broth

Prep. time: 15 min	Cook time: 240 min

DIRECTIONS

1. Combine all ingredients in a slow cooker.
2. Cook on low for 4 hours or until the barley is tender and the lamb is fully cooked.
3. Allow to cool before serving.

LAMB AND SWEET POTATO CASSEROLE

32% protein, 28% carbohydrates, 25% fat, 7% minerals, 5% fiber, 2% cholesterol, 1% sodium, 0.5% potassium
Total Calories: 900 kcal (1.18 kcal/g, 33.5 kcal/oz)
Total Recipe Amount: 27 oz (765 g)

INGREDIENTS

- 2 cups cooked, shredded lamb
- 2 cups chopped sweet potatoes
- 1 cup chopped carrots
- 1 cup chopped green beans
- 1/2 cup peas
- 2 cups low-sodium lamb broth

Prep. time: 15 min   Cook time: 240 min

DIRECTIONS

1. Combine all ingredients in a slow cooker.
2. Cook on low for 4 hours or until the sweet potatoes are tender and the lamb is fully cooked.
3. Allow to cool before serving.

LAMB AND VEGETABLE MEDLEY

28% protein, 32% carbohydrates, 18% fat, 10% minerals, 7% fiber, 3% cholesterol, 2% sodium, 2% potassium
Total Calories: 850 kcal (1.11 kcal/g, 31.4 kcal/oz)
Total Recipe Amount: 27 oz (765 g)

INGREDIENTS

- 2 cups cooked, shredded lamb
- 2 cups chopped carrots
- 1 cup chopped sweet potatoes
- 1 cup chopped green beans
- 1/2 cup peas
- 2 cups low-sodium lamb broth

Prep. time: 10 min   Cook time: 240 min

DIRECTIONS

1. Combine all ingredients in a slow cooker.
2. Cook on low for 4 hours or until the vegetables are tender and the lamb is fully cooked.
3. Allow to cool before serving.

VENISON AND APPLE RAGOUT

32% protein, 28% carbohydrates, 25% fat, 7% minerals, 5% fiber, 2% cholesterol, 1% sodium, 0.5% potassium
Total Calories: 850 kcal (1.11 kcal/g, 31.4 kcal/oz)
Total Recipe Amount: 27 oz (765 g)

INGREDIENTS

| Prep. time: 15 min | Cook time: 240 min |

- 2 cups cooked, shredded venison
- 2 cups chopped apples
- 1 cup chopped carrots
- 1 cup chopped green beans
- 1/2 cup peas
- 2 cups low-sodium venison broth

DIRECTIONS

1. Combine all ingredients in a slow cooker.
2. Cook on low for 4 hours or the carrots and apples are tender and the venison is fully cooked.
3. Allow to cool before serving.

VENISON AND SWEET POTATO CASSEROLE

30% protein, 30% carbohydrates, 20% fat, 10% minerals, 5% fiber, 2% cholesterol, 2% sodium, 1% potassium
Total Calories: 870 kcal (1.14 kcal/g, 32.3 kcal/oz)
Total Recipe Amount: 27 oz (765 g)

INGREDIENTS

| Prep. time: 15 min | Cook time: 240 min |

- 2 cups cooked, shredded venison
- 2 cups chopped sweet potatoes
- 1 cup chopped carrots
- 1 cup chopped green beans
- 1/2 cup peas
- 2 cups low-sodium venison broth

DIRECTIONS

1. Combine all ingredients in a slow cooker.
2. Cook on low for 4 hours or until the sweet potatoes are tender and the venison is fully cooked.
3. Allow to cool before serving.

VENISON AND PEAR PORRIDGE

30% protein, 30% carbohydrates, 20% fat, 10% minerals, 5% fiber, 2% cholesterol, 2% sodium, 1% potassium
Total Calories: 820 kcal (1.07 kcal/g, 30.36 kcal/oz)
Total Recipe Amount: 27 oz (765 g)

INGREDIENTS

Prep. time: 15 min   Cook time: 240 min

- 2 cups cooked, shredded venison
- 2 cups chopped pears
- 1 cup cooked quinoa
- 1 cup chopped carrots
- 1/2 cup peas
- 2 cups low-sodium venison broth

DIRECTIONS

1. Combine all ingredients in a slow cooker.
2. Cook on low for 4 hours or until the carrots and pears are tender and the venison is fully cooked.
3. Allow to cool before serving.

PUMPKIN AND LENTIL STEW

28% protein, 32% carbohydrates, 18% fat, 10% minerals, 7% fiber, 3% cholesterol, 2% sodium, 2% potassium
Total Calories: 780 kcal (1.02 kcal/g, 28.93 kcal/oz)
Total Recipe Amount: 27 oz (765 g)

INGREDIENTS

Prep. time: 10 min   Cook time: 240 min

- 1 cup cooked lentils
- 2 cups pumpkin puree
- 1 cup chopped carrots
- 1 cup chopped spinach
- 1/2 cup peas
- 2 cups low-sodium vegetable broth

DIRECTIONS

1. Combine all ingredients in a slow cooker.
2. Cook on low for 4 hours or until the lentils are tender and the vegetables is fully cooked.
3. Allow to cool before serving.

SWEET POTATO AND QUINOA CASSEROLE

30% protein, 30% carbohydrates, 20% fat, 10% minerals, 5% fiber, 2% cholesterol, 2% sodium, 1% potassium
Total Calories: 850 kcal (1.11 kcal/g, 31.4 kcal/oz)
Total Recipe Amount: 27 oz (765 g)

INGREDIENTS

- 2 cups cooked quinoa
- 2 cups chopped sweet potatoes
- 1 cup chopped carrots
- 1 cup chopped green beans
- 1/2 cup peas
- 2 cups low-sodium vegetable broth

Prep. time: 15 min   Cook time: 240 min

DIRECTIONS

1. Combine all ingredients in a slow cooker.
2. Cook on low for 4 hours or until the quinoa is tender and the sweet potatoes are fully cooked.
3. Allow to cool before serving.

VEGETABLE MEDLEY

28% protein, 32% carbohydrates, 18% fat, 10% minerals, 7% fiber, 3% cholesterol, 2% sodium, 2% potassium
Total Calories: 800 kcal (1.04 kcal/g, 29.5 kcal/oz)
Total Recipe Amount: 27 oz (765 g)

INGREDIENTS

- 2 cups chopped carrots
- 2 cups chopped green beans
- 1 cup chopped sweet potatoes
- 1 cup peas
- 2 cups low-sodium vegetable broth

Prep. time: 10 min   Cook time: 240 min

DIRECTIONS

1. Combine all ingredients in a slow cooker.
2. Cook on low for 4 hours or until the vegetables are tender and the sweet potatoes are fully cooked.
3. Allow to cool before serving.

FROZEN

CHICKEN AND BROCCOLI BARS

24% protein, 28% carbohydrates, 12% fat, 14% minerals, 8% fiber, 5% cholesterol, 5% sodium, 4% potassium
Total Calories: 320 kcal (1.13 kcal/g, 32.0 kcal/oz)
Total Recipe Amount: 10 oz (283.5 g)

INGREDIENTS

- 1 cup cooked chicken breast, chopped
- 1/2 cup cooked broccoli, chopped
- 1/4 cup rolled oats
- 1/4 cup unsweetened applesauce

Prep. time: 15 min   Cook time: 0 min

DIRECTIONS

1. Combine the chopped chicken, broccoli, rolled oats, and applesauce in a large mixing bowl. Mix until well combined.
2. Spoon the mixture into silicone molds or a baking dish and freeze for at least 2 hours before serving.

TURKEY AND BLUEBERRY POPS

22% protein, 32% carbohydrates, 12% fat, 15% minerals, 7% fiber, 7% cholesterol, 3% sodium, 2% potassium
Total Calories: 340 kcal (1.21 kcal/g, 34.0 kcal/oz)
Total Recipe Amount: 10 oz (283.5 g)

INGREDIENTS

- 1 cup cooked turkey breast, chopped
- 1/2 cup fresh blueberries
- 1/4 cup rolled oats
- 1/4 cup unsweetened applesauce

Prep. time: 15 min   Cook time: 0 min

DIRECTIONS

1. Combine the chopped turkey, blueberries, rolled oats, and applesauce in a large mixing bowl. Mix until well combined.
2. Spoon the mixture into popsicle molds and freeze for at least 2 hours before serving.

DUCK AND GREEN BEAN POPS

26% protein, 28% carbohydrates, 12% fat, 14% minerals, 8% fiber, 6% cholesterol, 4% sodium, 2% potassium
Total Calories: 310 kcal (1.11 kcal/g, 31.0 kcal/oz)
Total Recipe Amount: 10 oz (283.5 g)

INGREDIENTS

- 1 cup cooked duck breast, chopped
- 1/2 cup cooked green beans, chopped
- 1/4 cup rolled oats
- 1 tbsp chia seeds

Prep. time: 15 min   Cook time: 0 min

DIRECTIONS

1. Combine the chopped duck, green beans, rolled oats, and chia seeds in a large mixing bowl. Mix until well combined.
2. Spoon the mixture into popsicle molds and freeze for at least 2 hours before serving.

BEEF AND SPINACH FREEZIES

24% protein, 30% carbohydrates, 10% fat, 15% minerals, 8% fiber, 5% cholesterol, 4% sodium, 4% potassium
Total Calories: 320 kcal (1.13 kcal/g, 32.0 kcal/oz)
Total Recipe Amount: 10 oz (283.5 g)

INGREDIENTS

- 1 cup cooked beef, chopped
- 1/2 cup fresh spinach, chopped
- 1/4 cup rolled oats
- 1 tbsp flaxseed meal

Prep. time: 15 min   Cook time: 0 min

DIRECTIONS

1. Combine the chopped beef, spinach, rolled oats, and flaxseed meal in a large mixing bowl. Mix until well combined.
2. Spoon the mixture into silicone molds and freeze for at least 2 hours before serving.

PORK AND PEAR SORBET

20% protein, 34% carbohydrates, 10% fat, 16% minerals, 9% fiber, 5% cholesterol, 3% sodium, 3% potassium
Total Calories: 300 kcal (1.06 kcal/g, 30.0 kcal/oz)
Total Recipe Amount: 10 oz (283.5 g)

INGREDIENTS

- 1 cup cooked pork, chopped
- 1/2 cup pear, chopped
- 1/4 cup rolled oats
- 1/4 cup unsweetened applesauce

Prep. time: 15 min	Cook time: 0 min

DIRECTIONS

1. Combine the chopped pork, pear, rolled oats, and applesauce in a large mixing bowl. Mix until well combined.
2. Spoon the mixture into silicone molds and freeze for at least 2 hours before serving.

FISH AND KALE POPS

22% protein, 36% carbohydrates, 12% fat, 14% minerals, 6% fiber, 5% cholesterol, 3% sodium, 2% potassium
Total Calories: 310 kcal (1.11 kcal/g, 31.0 kcal/oz)
Total Recipe Amount: 10 oz (283.5 g)

INGREDIENTS

- 1 cup cooked white fish, chopped
- 1/2 cup fresh kale, chopped
- 1/4 cup rolled oats
- 1 tbsp flaxseed meal

Prep. time: 15 min	Cook time: 0 min

DIRECTIONS

1. Combine the chopped fish, kale, rolled oats, and flaxseed meal in a large mixing bowl. Mix until well combined.
2. Spoon the mixture into popsicle molds and freeze for at least 2 hours before serving.

LIVER AND STRAWBERRY CUBES

24% protein, 34% carbohydrates, 12% fat, 14% minerals, 6% fiber, 5% cholesterol, 3% sodium, 2% potassium
Total Calories: 320 kcal (1.13 kcal/g, 32.0 kcal/oz)
Total Recipe Amount: 10 oz (283.5 g)

INGREDIENTS

- 1 cup cooked liver, chopped
- 1/2 cup fresh strawberries, chopped
- 1/4 cup rolled oats
- 1/4 cup unsweetened applesauce

Prep. time: 15 min   Cook time: 0 min

DIRECTIONS

1. Combine the chopped liver, strawberries, rolled oats, and applesauce in a large mixing bowl. Mix until well combined.
2. Spoon the mixture into silicone molds and freeze for at least 2 hours before serving.

LAMB AND PINEAPPLE ICE CREAM

22% protein, 30% carbohydrates, 10% fat, 16% minerals, 9% fiber, 5% cholesterol, 3% sodium, 5% potassium
Total Calories: 300 kcal (1.06 kcal/g, 30.0 kcal/oz)
Total Recipe Amount: 10 oz (283.5 g)

INGREDIENTS

- 1 cup cooked lamb, chopped
- 1/2 cup fresh pineapple, chopped
- 1/4 cup rolled oats
- 1/4 cup unsweetened applesauce

Prep. time: 15 min   Cook time: 0 min

DIRECTIONS

1. Combine the chopped lamb, pineapple, rolled oats, and applesauce in a large mixing bowl. Mix until well combined.
2. Spoon the mixture into silicone molds and freeze for at least 2 hours before serving.

VENISON AND SWEET CORN CREAMS

24% protein, 30% carbohydrates, 14% fat, 14% minerals, 6% fiber, 5% cholesterol, 4% sodium, 3% potassium
Total Calories: 330 kcal (1.16 kcal/g, 33.0 kcal/oz)
Total Recipe Amount: 10 oz (283.5 g)

INGREDIENTS

- 1 cup cooked venison, chopped
- 1/2 cup sweet corn kernels
- 1/4 cup rolled oats
- 1/4 cup unsweetened applesauce

Prep. time: 15 min	Cook time: 0 min

DIRECTIONS

1. Combine the chopped venison, sweet corn, rolled oats, and applesauce in a large mixing bowl. Mix until well combined.
2. Spoon the mixture into silicone molds and freeze for at least 2 hours before serving.

YOGURT AND BERRY POPS

18% protein, 50% carbohydrates, 10% fat, 12% minerals, 5% fiber, 3% cholesterol, 1% sodium, 1% potassium
Total Calories: 290 kcal (1.02 kcal/g, 29.0 kcal/oz)
Total Recipe Amount: 10 oz (283.5 g)

INGREDIENTS

- 1 cup plain yogurt
- 1/2 cup mixed berries (blueberries, strawberries, raspberries), chopped

Prep. time: 10 min	Cook time: 0 min

DIRECTIONS

1. Combine the yogurt and mixed berries in a large mixing bowl. Mix until well combined.
2. Spoon the mixture into popsicle molds and freeze for at least 2 hours before serving.

APPLE AND CARROT CUBES

10% protein, 60% carbohydrates, 5% fat, 10% minerals, 8% fiber, 2% cholesterol, 3% sodium, 2% potassium
Total Calories: 280 kcal (0.99 kcal/g, 28.0 kcal/oz)
Total Recipe Amount: 10 oz (283.5 g)

INGREDIENTS

Prep. time: 10 min	Cook time: 0 min

- 1/2 cup grated apple
- 1/2 cup grated carrot
- 1/4 cup rolled oats
- 1/4 cup unsweetened applesauce

DIRECTIONS

1. Combine the grated apple, carrot, rolled oats, and applesauce in a large mixing bowl. Mix until well combined.
2. Spoon the mixture into silicone molds and freeze for at least 2 hours before serving.

PUMPKIN AND PEANUT BUTTER FREEZIES

22% protein, 40% carbohydrates, 15% fat, 10% minerals, 7% fiber, 3% cholesterol, 2% sodium, 1% potassium
Total Calories: 310 kcal (1.11 kcal/g, 31.0 kcal/oz)
Total Recipe Amount: 10 oz (280.5 g)

INGREDIENTS

Prep. time: 10 min	Cook time: 0 min

- 1/2 cup pumpkin puree
- 1/4 cup peanut butter (unsalted, xylitol-free)
- 1/4 cup rolled oats
- 1/4 cup unsweetened applesauce

DIRECTIONS

1. Combine the pumpkin puree, peanut butter, rolled oats, and applesauce in a large mixing bowl. Mix until well combined.
2. Spoon the mixture into silicone molds and freeze for at least 2 hours before serving.

WATERMELON AND MINT SORBET

4% protein, 84% carbohydrates, 0% fat, 5% minerals, 5% fiber, 1% cholesterol, 0% sodium, 1% potassium
Total Calories: 160 kcal (0.56 kcal/g, 16.0 kcal/oz)
Total Recipe Amount: 10 oz (283.5 g)

INGREDIENTS

- 1 cup watermelon, chopped
- 1 tbsp fresh mint, chopped
- 1/4 cup water

Prep. time: 10 min	Cook time: 0 min

DIRECTIONS

1. Combine the chopped watermelon, fresh mint, and water in a blender. Blend until smooth.
2. Pour the mixture into a baking dish and freeze for at least 2 hours before serving.

SWEET POTATO AND COCONUT CREAMS

18% protein, 50% carbohydrates, 20% fat, 8% minerals, 4% fiber, 2% cholesterol, 2% sodium, 1% potassium
Total Calories: 340 kcal (1.21 kcal/g, 34.0 kcal/oz)
Total Recipe Amount: 10 oz (283.5 g)

INGREDIENTS

- 1/2 cup cooked sweet potato, mashed
- 1/4 cup coconut milk
- 1/4 cup rolled oats
- 1/4 cup unsweetened applesauce

Prep. time: 10 min	Cook time: 0 min

DIRECTIONS

1. Combine the mashed sweet potato, coconut milk, rolled oats, and applesauce in a large mixing bowl. Mix until well combined.
2. Spoon the mixture into silicone molds and freeze for at least 2 hours before serving.

SPECIAL DIETS

GRAIN-FREE DUCK AND BUTTERNUT SQUASH BITES

29% protein, 32% carbohydrates, 11% fat, 7% minerals, 5% fiber, 3% cholesterol, 7% sodium, 6% potassium
Total Calories: 370 kcal (1.31 kcal/g, 37.0 kcal/oz)
Total Recipe Amount: 10 oz (283.5 g)

INGREDIENTS

- 1 cup cooked duck, chopped
- 1 cup cooked butternut squash, mashed
- 1 egg
- 1/2 cup coconut flour

Prep. time: 15 min   Cook time: 30 min

DIRECTIONS

1. Preheat your oven to 350°F (175°C).
2. Combine the chopped duck, mashed butternut squash, and egg in a mixing bowl. Mix until well combined.
3. Gradually add the coconut flour to the mixture until it forms a dough-like consistency.
4. Roll the mixture into bite-sized balls and place them on a baking sheet lined with parchment paper.
5. Bake for 30 minutes or until the bites are firm and slightly golden.

GRAIN-FREE PORK AND ZUCCHINI BITES

28% protein, 30% carbohydrates, 12% fat, 7% minerals, 5% fiber, 3% cholesterol, 8% sodium, 7% potassium
Total Calories: 380 kcal (1.35 kcal/g, 38.0 kcal/oz)
Total Recipe Amount: 10 oz (283.5 g)

INGREDIENTS

- 1 cup cooked pork, chopped
- 1 cup cooked zucchini, mashed
- 1 egg
- 1/2 cup almond flour

Prep. time: 15 min   Cook time: 30 min

DIRECTIONS

1. Preheat your oven to 350°F (175°C).
2. Combine the chopped pork, mashed zucchini, and egg in a mixing bowl. Mix until well combined.
3. Gradually add the almond flour to the mixture until it forms a dough-like consistency.
4. Roll the mixture into bite-sized balls and place them on a baking sheet lined with parchment paper.
5. Bake for 30 minutes or until the bites are firm and slightly golden.

GRAIN-FREE RABBIT AND SPINACH COOKIES

28% protein, 30% carbohydrates, 12% fat, 7% minerals, 5% fiber, 3% cholesterol, 8% sodium, 7% potassium
Total Calories: 380 kcal (1.35 kcal/g, 38.0 kcal/oz)
Total Recipe Amount: 10 oz (283.5 g)

INGREDIENTS

- 1 cup cooked rabbit, chopped
- 1 cup cooked spinach, chopped
- 1 egg
- 1/2 cup almond flour

Prep. time: 15 min   Cook time: 30 min

DIRECTIONS

1. Preheat your oven to 350°F (175°C).
2. Combine the chopped rabbit, spinach, and egg in a mixing bowl. Mix until well combined.
3. Gradually add the almond flour to the mixture until it forms a dough-like consistency.
4. Form the mixture into small cookies and place them on a baking sheet lined with parchment paper.
5. Bake for 30 minutes or until the cookies are firm and slightly golden.

LOW-FAT BEEF AND VEGETABLE SOUP

18% protein, 52% carbohydrates, 6% fat, 7% minerals, 5% fiber, 3% cholesterol, 5% sodium, 4% potassium
Total Calories: 200 kcal (0.56 kcal/g, 16.0 kcal/oz)
Total Recipe Amount: 12.5 oz (354 g)

INGREDIENTS

- 1/2 cup lean ground beef
- 1 cup chopped carrots
- 1 cup chopped green beans
- 2 cups low-sodium chicken broth

Prep. time: 15 min   Cook time: 30 min

DIRECTIONS

1. In a large pot, brown the ground beef over medium heat until fully cooked. Drain any excess fat.
2. Add the chopped carrots, green beans, and chicken broth to the pot.
3. Bring the mixture to a boil, then reduce the heat and simmer for 20-25 minutes or until the vegetables are tender.
4. Allow the soup to cool before serving it to your dog. Any leftovers can be stored in the refrigerator for up to three days.

LOW-FAT COD AND OATMEAL COOKIES

20% protein, 50% carbohydrates, 5% fat, 8% minerals, 7% fiber, 2% cholesterol, 4% sodium, 4% potassium
Total Calories: 290 kcal (1.19 kcal/g, 33.7 kcal/oz)
Total Recipe Amount: 8.6 oz (243 g)

INGREDIENTS

- 1 cup cooked cod, flaked
- 1 cup cooked oatmeal
- 1 egg white

Prep. time: 15 min   Cook time: 20 min

DIRECTIONS

1. Preheat your oven to 350°F (175°C).
2. Combine the cod, oatmeal, and egg white in a mixing bowl. Mix until well combined.
3. Form the mixture into small cookies and place them on a baking sheet lined with parchment paper.
4. Bake for 20 minutes or until the cookies are firm and slightly golden. Allow to cool before serving.

LOW-FAT SWEET POTATO AND APPLE PATTIES

10% protein, 60% carbohydrates, 5% fat, 10% minerals, 8% fiber, 2% cholesterol, 3% sodium, 2% potassium
Total Calories: 400 kcal (1.1 kcal/g, 28.5 kcal/oz)
Total Recipe Amount: 14 oz (387 g)

INGREDIENTS

- 1 cup mashed sweet potatoes
- 1/2 cup finely chopped apples (ensure no seeds or core)
- 1/2 cup whole wheat flour
- 1 egg
- 1 tbsp olive oil

Prep. time: 15 min   Cook time: 20 min

DIRECTIONS

1. Preheat your oven to 350°F (175°C) and line a baking sheet with parchment paper.
2. In a large bowl, mix the mashed sweet potatoes, chopped apples, whole wheat flour, egg, and olive oil until well combined.
3. Form the mixture into small patties, about 1/4 cup each, and place them on the prepared baking sheet.
4. Bake for 20 minutes, flipping halfway through, until the patties are golden brown and firm.

HYPOALLERGENIC LAMB AND QUINOA

18% protein, 40% carbohydrates, 10% fat, 5% minerals, 5% fiber, 5% cholesterol, 7% sodium, 10% potassium
Total Calories: 400 kcal (1.76 kcal/g, 50.0 kcal/oz)
Total Recipe Amount: 8 oz (227 g)

INGREDIENTS

- 1 cup cooked lamb, chopped
- 1 cup cooked quinoa
- 1 tbsp coconut oil

Prep. time: 15 min   Cook time: 30 min

DIRECTIONS

1. Preheat your oven to 350°F (175°C).
2. Combine the lamb, quinoa, and coconut oil in a mixing bowl. Mix until well combined.
3. Roll the mixture into bite-sized balls and place them on a baking sheet lined with parchment paper.
4. Bake for 30 minutes or until the bites are firm and slightly golden. Allow to cool before serving.

HYPOALLERGENIC VENISON AND RICE

25% protein, 35% carbohydrates, 10% fat, 6% minerals, 5% fiber, 5% cholesterol, 7% sodium, 7% potassium
Total Calories: 410 kcal (1.86 kcal/g, 53.2 kcal/oz)
Total Recipe Amount: 7.7 oz (220 g)

INGREDIENTS

- 1 cup cooked venison, chopped
- 1 cup cooked rice
- 1 egg

Prep. time: 20 min   Cook time: 40 min

DIRECTIONS

1. Preheat your oven to 350°F (175°C).
2. Combine the venison, rice, and egg in a mixing bowl. Mix until well combined.
3. Roll the mixture into bite-sized balls and place them on a baking sheet lined with parchment paper.
4. Bake for 40 minutes or until the bites are firm and slightly golden. Allow to cool before serving.

HYPOALLERGENIC BISON AND PEA MIX

25% protein, 35% carbohydrates, 12% fat, 5% minerals, 5% fiber, 5% cholesterol, 6% sodium, 7% potassium
Total Calories: 420 kcal (1.95 kcal/g, 55.3 kcal/oz)
Total Recipe Amount: 7.6 oz (215 g)

INGREDIENTS

| Prep. time: 15 min | Cook time: 35 min |

- 1 cup cooked bison, chopped
- 1 cup cooked peas, mashed
- 1 tbsp flaxseed oil

DIRECTIONS

1. Preheat your oven to 350°F (175°C).
2. Combine the bison, mashed peas, and flaxseed oil in a mixing bowl. Mix until well combined.
3. Roll the mixture into bite-sized balls and place them on a baking sheet lined with parchment paper.
4. Bake for 35 minutes or until the bites are firm and slightly golden. Allow to cool before serving.

HYPOALLERGENIC QUAIL AND GREEN BEANS

25% protein, 30% carbohydrates, 12% fat, 6% minerals, 5% fiber, 5% cholesterol, 7% sodium, 10% potassium
Total Calories: 380 kcal (1.90 kcal/g, 54.3 kcal/oz)
Total Recipe Amount: 7 oz (200 g)

INGREDIENTS

| Prep. time: 15 min | Cook time: 35 min |

- 1 cup cooked quail, chopped
- 1 cup cooked green beans, mashed
- 1 tbsp olive oil

DIRECTIONS

1. Preheat your oven to 350°F (175°C).
2. Combine the quail, mashed green beans, and olive oil in a mixing bowl. Mix until well combined.
3. Roll the mixture into bite-sized balls and place them on a baking sheet lined with parchment paper.
4. Bake for 35 minutes or until the bites are firm and slightly golden. Allow to cool before serving.

HOLIDAY TREATS

BIRTHDAY VENISON AND APPLE CAKE

24% protein, 35% carbohydrates, 12% fat, 10% minerals, 7% fiber, 3% cholesterol, 5% sodium, 4% potassium
Total Calories: 320 kcal (1.13 kcal/g, 32.0 kcal/oz)
Total Recipe Amount: 10 oz (283.5 g)

INGREDIENTS

- 1 cup cooked venison, chopped
- 1/2 cup grated apple
- 1 egg
- 1/4 cup oat flour
- 1/4 cup rolled oats

Prep. time: 20 min	Cook time: 25 min

DIRECTIONS

1. Preheat your oven to 350°F (175°C).
2. Combine the chopped venison, grated apple, and egg in a large mixing bowl. Mix until well combined.
3. Gradually add the oat flour and rolled oats to the mixture, stirring until a dough forms.
4. Press the mixture into a greased baking dish and bake for 25 minutes or until firm and golden.
5. Let cool before serving.

VALENTINE'S DAY DUCK AND STRAWBERRY HEARTS

26% protein, 34% carbohydrates, 15% fat, 10% minerals, 5% fiber, 3% cholesterol, 5% sodium, 2% potassium
Total Calories: 340 kcal (1.20 kcal/g, 34.0 kcal/oz)
Total Recipe Amount: 10 oz (283.5 g)

INGREDIENTS

- 1 cup cooked duck breast, chopped
- 1/2 cup fresh strawberries, chopped
- 1 egg
- 1/4 cup oat flour
- 1/4 cup rolled oats

Prep. time: 15 min	Cook time: 30 min

DIRECTIONS

1. Preheat your oven to 350°F (175°C).
2. Combine the chopped duck, strawberries, and egg in a large mixing bowl. Mix until well combined.
3. Gradually add the oat flour and rolled oats to the mixture, stirring until a dough forms.
4. Shape the mixture into heart shapes and place them on a baking sheet lined with parchment paper.
5. Bake for 30 minutes or until the hearts are firm and slightly golden.

VALENTINE'S DAY BEEF AND BEET TREATS

28% protein, 30% carbohydrates, 12% fat, 10% minerals, 8% fiber, 5% cholesterol, 4% sodium, 3% potassium
Total Calories: 350 kcal (1.24 kcal/g, 35.0 kcal/oz)
Total Recipe Amount: 10 oz (283.5 g)

INGREDIENTS

- 1 cup cooked beef, chopped
- 1/2 cup cooked beets, mashed
- 1 egg
- 1/4 cup oat flour
- 1/4 cup rolled oats

Prep. time: 20 min   Cook time: 25 min

DIRECTIONS

1. Preheat your oven to 350°F (175°C).
2. Combine the chopped beef, mashed beets, and egg in a large mixing bowl. Mix until well combined.
3. Gradually add the oat flour and rolled oats to the mixture, stirring until a dough forms.
4. Shape the mixture into heart shapes and place them on a baking sheet lined with parchment paper.
5. Bake for 30 minutes or until the treats are firm and slightly golden.

PATRICK'S DAY SALMON AND SPINACH SNACKS

22% protein, 35% carbohydrates, 12% fat, 10% minerals, 10% fiber, 4% cholesterol, 4% sodium, 3% potassium
Total Calories: 330 kcal (1.16 kcal/g, 33.0 kcal/oz)
Total Recipe Amount: 10 oz (283.5 g)

INGREDIENTS

- 1 cup cooked salmon, flaked
- 1/2 cup fresh spinach, chopped
- 1 egg
- 1/4 cup oat flour
- 1/4 cup rolled oats

Prep. time: 15 min   Cook time: 25 min

DIRECTIONS

1. Preheat your oven to 350°F (175°C).
2. Combine the flaked salmon, chopped spinach, and egg in a large mixing bowl. Mix until well combined.
3. Gradually add the oat flour and rolled oats to the mixture, stirring until a dough forms.
4. Shape the mixture into small snacks and place them on a baking sheet lined with parchment paper.
5. Bake for 25 minutes or until the snacks are firm and slightly golden.

EASTER LAMB AND CARROT MEDLEY

26% protein, 34% carbohydrates, 10% fat, 8% minerals, 10% fiber, 4% cholesterol, 4% sodium, 4% potassium
Total Calories: 310 kcal (1.10 kcal/g, 31.0 kcal/oz)
Total Recipe Amount: 10 oz (283.5 g)

INGREDIENTS

- 1 cup cooked lamb, chopped
- 1/2 cup grated carrot
- 1 egg
- 1/4 cup oat flour
- 1/4 cup rolled oats

Prep. time: 20 min   Cook time: 25 min

DIRECTIONS

1. Preheat your oven to 350°F (175°C).
2. Combine the chopped lamb, grated carrot, and egg in a large mixing bowl. Mix until well combined.
3. Gradually add the oat flour and rolled oats to the mixture, stirring until a dough forms.
4. Shape the mixture into medley shapes and place them on a baking sheet lined with parchment paper.
5. Bake for 30 minutes or until the medleys are firm and slightly golden.

EASTER BEEF AND CARROT BUNNIES

28% protein, 30% carbohydrates, 12% fat, 10% minerals, 8% fiber, 5% cholesterol, 4% sodium, 3% potassium
Total Calories: 350 kcal (1.24 kcal/g, 35.0 kcal/oz)
Total Recipe Amount: 10 oz (283.5 g)

INGREDIENTS

- 1 cup cooked beef, chopped
- 1/2 cup grated carrot
- 1 egg
- 1/4 cup oat flour
- 1/4 cup rolled oats

Prep. time: 15 min   Cook time: 30 min

DIRECTIONS

1. Preheat your oven to 350°F (175°C).
2. Combine the chopped beef, grated carrot, and egg in a large mixing bowl. Mix until well combined.
3. Gradually add the oat flour and rolled oats to the mixture, stirring until a dough forms.
4. Shape the mixture into bunny shapes and place them on a baking sheet lined with parchment paper.
5. Bake for 30 minutes or until the bunnies are firm and slightly golden.

PRIDE FISH AND MANGO DELIGHT

20% protein, 40% carbohydrates, 15% fat, 10% minerals, 8% fiber, 3% cholesterol, 2% sodium, 2% potassium
Total Calories: 300 kcal (1.06 kcal/g, 30.0 kcal/oz)
Total Recipe Amount: 10 oz (283.5 g)

INGREDIENTS

- 1 cup cooked white fish, flaked
- 1/2 cup diced fresh mango
- 1 tbsp olive oil
- 1 tsp chopped fresh cilantro

Prep. time: 15 min   Cook time: 10 min

DIRECTIONS

1. Combine the flaked fish, diced mango, olive oil, and cilantro in a large mixing bowl. Mix until well combined.
2. Serve chilled or slightly warmed.

INDEPENDENCE DAY CHICKEN AND BLUEBERRY BITES

24% protein, 35% carbohydrates, 12% fat, 10% minerals, 8% fiber, 4% cholesterol, 4% sodium, 3% potassium
Total Calories: 320 kcal (1.13 kcal/g, 32.0 kcal/oz)
Total Recipe Amount: 10 oz (283.5 g)

INGREDIENTS

- 1 cup cooked chicken breast, chopped
- 1/2 cup fresh blueberries
- 1 egg
- 1/4 cup oat flour
- 1/4 cup rolled oats

Prep. time: 15 min   Cook time: 30 min

DIRECTIONS

1. Preheat your oven to 350°F (175°C).
2. Combine the chopped chicken, blueberries, and egg in a large mixing bowl. Mix until well combined.
3. Gradually add the oat flour and rolled oats to the mixture, stirring until a dough forms.
4. Shape the mixture into bite-sized pieces and place them on a baking sheet lined with parchment paper.
5. Bake for 30 minutes or until the bites are firm and slightly golden.

INDEPENDENCE DAY BEEF AND BLUEBERRY STARS

26% protein, 34% carbohydrates, 12% fat, 10% minerals, 8% fiber, 4% cholesterol, 4% sodium, 2% potassium
Total Calories: 340 kcal (1.20 kcal/g, 34.0 kcal/oz)
Total Recipe Amount: 10 oz (283.5 g)

INGREDIENTS

- 1 cup cooked beef, chopped
- 1/2 cup fresh blueberries
- 1 egg
- 1/4 cup oat flour
- 1/4 cup rolled oats

Prep. time: 15 min   Cook time: 30 min

DIRECTIONS

1. Preheat your oven to 350°F (175°C).
2. Combine the chopped beef, blueberries, and egg in a large mixing bowl. Mix until well combined.
3. Gradually add the oat flour and rolled oats to the mixture, stirring until a dough forms.
4. Shape the mixture into star shapes and place them on a baking sheet lined with parchment paper.
5. Bake for 30 minutes or until the stars are firm and slightly golden.

HALLOWEEN PUMPKIN AND APPLE COOKIES

22% protein, 40% carbohydrates, 12% fat, 10% minerals, 8% fiber, 4% cholesterol, 4% sodium, 2% potassium
Total Calories: 300 kcal (1.06 kcal/g, 30.0 kcal/oz)
Total Recipe Amount: 10 oz (283.5 g)

INGREDIENTS

- 1 cup pumpkin puree
- 1/2 cup grated apple
- 1 egg
- 1/4 cup oat flour
- 1/4 cup rolled oats

Prep. time: 15 min   Cook time: 25 min

DIRECTIONS

1. Preheat your oven to 350°F (175°C).
2. Combine the pumpkin puree, grated apple, and egg in a large mixing bowl. Mix until well combined.
3. Gradually add the oat flour and rolled oats to the mixture, stirring until a dough forms.
4. Shape the mixture into cookie shapes and place them on a baking sheet lined with parchment paper.
5. Bake for 25 minutes or until the cookies are firm and slightly golden.

HALLOWEEN FISH AND PUMPKIN GHOSTS

24% protein, 35% carbohydrates, 12% fat, 10% minerals, 8% fiber, 4% cholesterol, 4% sodium, 3% potassium
Total Calories: 320 kcal (1.13 kcal/g, 32.0 kcal/oz)
Total Recipe Amount: 10 oz (283.5 g)

INGREDIENTS

- 1 cup cooked white fish, chopped
- 1/2 cup pumpkin puree
- 1 egg
- 1/4 cup oat flour
- 1/4 cup rolled oats

Prep. time: 15 min   Cook time: 30 min

DIRECTIONS

1. Preheat your oven to 350°F (175°C).
2. Combine the chopped fish, pumpkin puree, and egg in a large mixing bowl. Mix until well combined.
3. Gradually add the oat flour and rolled oats to the mixture, stirring until a dough forms.
4. Shape the mixture into ghost shapes and place them on a baking sheet lined with parchment paper.
5. Bake for 30 minutes or until the ghosts are firm and slightly golden.

THANKSGIVING CHICKEN AND SWEET POTATO FEAST

26% protein, 34% carbohydrates, 10% fat, 8% minerals, 10% fiber, 4% cholesterol, 4% sodium, 4% potassium
Total Calories: 310 kcal (1.10 kcal/g, 31.0 kcal/oz)
Total Recipe Amount: 10 oz (283.5 g)

INGREDIENTS

- 1 cup cooked chicken breast, chopped
- 1/2 cup cooked sweet potato, mashed
- 1 egg
- 1/4 cup oat flour
- 1/4 cup rolled oats

Prep. time: 15 min   Cook time: 30 min

DIRECTIONS

1. Preheat your oven to 350°F (175°C).
2. Combine the chopped chicken, mashed sweet potato, and egg in a large mixing bowl. Mix until well combined.
3. Gradually add the oat flour and rolled oats to the mixture, stirring until a dough forms.
4. Shape the mixture into small feasts and place them on a baking sheet lined with parchment paper.
5. Bake for 30 minutes or until the feasts are firm and slightly golden.

THANKSGIVING PORK AND SWEET POTATO PIES

28% protein, 30% carbohydrates, 12% fat, 10% minerals, 8% fiber, 5% cholesterol, 4% sodium, 3% potassium
Total Calories: 350 kcal (1.24 kcal/g, 35.0 kcal/oz)
Total Recipe Amount: 10 oz (283.5 g)

INGREDIENTS

- 1 cup cooked pork, chopped
- 1/2 cup cooked sweet potato, mashed
- 1 egg
- 1/4 cup oat flour
- 1/4 cup rolled oats

Prep. time: 15 min   Cook time: 30 min

DIRECTIONS

1. Preheat your oven to 350°F (175°C).
2. Combine the chopped pork, mashed sweet potato, and egg in a large mixing bowl. Mix until well combined.
3. Gradually add the oat flour and rolled oats to the mixture, stirring until a dough forms.
4. Shape the mixture into pie shapes and place them on a baking sheet lined with parchment paper.
5. Bake for 30 minutes or until the pies are firm and slightly golden.

HANUKKAH LAMB AND POTATO LATKES

26% protein, 34% carbohydrates, 10% fat, 8% minerals, 10% fiber, 4% cholesterol, 4% sodium, 4% potassium
Total Calories: 310 kcal (1.10 kcal/g, 31.0 kcal/oz)
Total Recipe Amount: 10 oz (283.5 g)

INGREDIENTS

- 1 cup cooked lamb, chopped
- 1/2 cup grated potato
- 1 egg
- 1/4 cup oat flour
- 1/4 cup rolled oats

Prep. time: 15 min   Cook time: 30 min

DIRECTIONS

1. Preheat your oven to 350°F (175°C).
2. Combine the chopped lamb, grated potato, and egg in a large mixing bowl. Mix until well combined.
3. Gradually add the oat flour and rolled oats to the mixture, stirring until a dough forms.
4. Shape the mixture into latkes and place them on a baking sheet lined with parchment paper.
5. Bake for 30 minutes or until the latkes are firm and slightly golden.

CHRISTMAS TURKEY AND CRANBERRY DELIGHT

24% protein, 35% carbohydrates, 12% fat, 10% minerals, 8% fiber, 4% cholesterol, 4% sodium, 3% potassium
Total Calories: 320 kcal (1.13 kcal/g, 32.0 kcal/oz)
Total Recipe Amount: 10 oz (283.5 g)

INGREDIENTS

- 1 cup cooked turkey breast, chopped
- 1/4 cup dried cranberries
- 1 egg
- 1/4 cup oat flour
- 1/4 cup rolled oats

Prep. time: 15 min   Cook time: 30 min

DIRECTIONS

1. Preheat your oven to 350°F (175°C).
2. Combine the chopped turkey, dried cranberries, and egg in a large mixing bowl. Mix until well combined.
3. Gradually add the oat flour and rolled oats to the mixture, stirring until a dough forms.
4. Shape the mixture into small delights and place them on a baking sheet lined with parchment paper.
5. Bake for 30 minutes or until the delights are firm and slightly golden.

CHRISTMAS TURKEY AND PUMPKIN COOKIES

26% protein, 34% carbohydrates, 12% fat, 10% minerals, 8% fiber, 4% cholesterol, 4% sodium, 2% potassium
Total Calories: 340 kcal (1.20 kcal/g, 34.0 kcal/oz)
Total Recipe Amount: 10 oz (283.5 g)

INGREDIENTS

- 1 cup cooked turkey breast, chopped
- 1/2 cup pumpkin puree
- 1 egg
- 1/4 cup oat flour
- 1/4 cup rolled oats

Prep. time: 15 min   Cook time: 30 min

DIRECTIONS

1. Preheat your oven to 350°F (175°C).
2. Combine the chopped turkey, pumpkin puree, and egg in a large mixing bowl. Mix until well combined.
3. Gradually add the oat flour and rolled oats to the mixture, stirring until a dough forms.
4. Shape the mixture into cookie shapes and place them on a baking sheet lined with parchment paper.
5. Bake for 25 minutes or until the cookies are firm and slightly golden.

NEW YEAR'S EVE BEEF AND SWEET PEA TREATS

28% protein, 30% carbohydrates, 12% fat, 10% minerals, 8% fiber, 5% cholesterol, 4% sodium, 3% potassium
Total Calories: 350 kcal (1.24 kcal/g, 35.0 kcal/oz)
Total Recipe Amount: 10 oz (283.5 g)

INGREDIENTS

- 1 cup cooked beef, chopped
- 1/2 cup cooked sweet peas
- 1 egg
- 1/4 cup oat flour
- 1/4 cup rolled oats

Prep. time: 15 min	Cook time: 30 min

DIRECTIONS

1. Preheat your oven to 350°F (175°C).
2. Combine the chopped beef, cooked peas, and egg in a large mixing bowl. Mix until well combined.
3. Gradually add the oat flour and rolled oats to the mixture, stirring until a dough forms.
4. Shape the mixture into small treats and place them on a baking sheet lined with parchment paper.
5. Bake for 30 minutes or until the treats are firm and slightly golden.

NEW YEAR'S EVE LAMB AND MINT BALLS

24% protein, 35% carbohydrates, 12% fat, 10% minerals, 8% fiber, 4% cholesterol, 4% sodium, 3% potassium
Total Calories: 320 kcal (1.13 kcal/g, 32.0 kcal/oz)
Total Recipe Amount: 10 oz (283.5 g)

INGREDIENTS

- 1 cup cooked lamb, chopped
- 1 tbsp fresh mint, chopped
- 1 egg
- 1/4 cup oat flour
- 1/4 cup rolled oats

Prep. time: 15 min	Cook time: 30 min

DIRECTIONS

1. Preheat your oven to 350°F (175°C).
2. Combine the chopped lamb, fresh mint, and egg in a large mixing bowl. Mix until well combined.
3. Gradually add the oat flour and rolled oats to the mixture, stirring until a dough forms.
4. Shape the mixture into bite-sized balls and place them on a baking sheet lined with parchment paper.
5. Bake for 30 minutes or until the balls are firm and slightly golden.

TRAINING TREATS

CHICKEN TRAINING BITES

26% protein, 34% carbohydrates, 10% fat, 7% minerals, 5% fiber, 3% cholesterol, 8% sodium, 7% potassium
Total Calories: 350 kcal (1.24 kcal/g, 35.0 kcal/oz)
Total Recipe Amount: 10 oz (283.5 g)

INGREDIENTS

- 1 cup cooked chicken breast, chopped
- 1 cup oat flour
- 1 egg

Prep. time: 15 min	Cook time: 30 min

DIRECTIONS

1. Preheat your oven to 350°F (175°C).
2. Combine the chopped chicken, oat flour, and egg in a mixing bowl. Mix until well combined.
3. Roll the mixture into bite-sized balls and place them on a baking sheet lined with parchment paper.
4. Bake for 30 minutes or until the bites are firm and slightly golden. Allow to cool before serving.

TURKEY TRAINING TREATS

24% protein, 36% carbohydrates, 12% fat, 8% minerals, 6% fiber, 5% cholesterol, 5% sodium, 4% potassium
Total Calories: 330 kcal (1.16 kcal/g, 33.0 kcal/oz)
Total Recipe Amount: 10 oz (283.5 g)

INGREDIENTS

- 1 cup cooked turkey breast, chopped
- 1 cup oat flour
- 1 egg

Prep. time: 15 min	Cook time: 30 min

DIRECTIONS

1. Preheat your oven to 350°F (175°C).
2. Combine the chopped turkey, oat flour, and egg in a mixing bowl. Mix until well combined.
3. Roll the mixture into bite-sized balls and place them on a baking sheet lined with parchment paper.
4. Bake for 30 minutes or until the treats are firm and slightly golden. Allow to cool before serving.

BEEF TRAINING BITES

28% protein, 32% carbohydrates, 15% fat, 10% minerals, 7% fiber, 5% cholesterol, 2% sodium, 1% potassium
Total Calories: 370 kcal (1.30 kcal/g, 37.0 kcal/oz)
Total Recipe Amount: 10 oz (283.5 g)

INGREDIENTS

- 1 cup cooked beef, chopped
- 1 cup oat flour
- 1 egg

Prep. time: 15 min   Cook time: 30 min

DIRECTIONS

1. Preheat your oven to 350°F (175°C).
2. Combine the chopped beef, oat flour, and egg in a mixing bowl. Mix until well combined.
3. Roll the mixture into bite-sized balls and place them on a baking sheet lined with parchment paper.
4. Bake for 30 minutes or until the bites are firm and slightly golden. Allow to cool before serving.

PORK TRAINING TREATS

25% protein, 35% carbohydrates, 12% fat, 10% minerals, 7% fiber, 5% cholesterol, 3% sodium, 3% potassium
Total Calories: 340 kcal (1.20 kcal/g, 34.0 kcal/oz)
Total Recipe Amount: 10 oz (283.5 g)

INGREDIENTS

- 1 cup cooked pork, chopped
- 1 cup oat flour
- 1 egg

Prep. time: 15 min   Cook time: 30 min

DIRECTIONS

1. Preheat your oven to 350°F (175°C).
2. Combine the chopped pork, oat flour, and egg in a mixing bowl. Mix until well combined.
3. Roll the mixture into bite-sized balls and place them on a baking sheet lined with parchment paper.
4. Bake for 30 minutes or until the treats are firm and slightly golden. Allow to cool before serving.

SALMON TRAINING BITES

26% protein, 34% carbohydrates, 14% fat, 8% minerals, 6% fiber, 4% cholesterol, 5% sodium, 3% potassium
Total Calories: 350 kcal (1.24 kcal/g, 35.0 kcal/oz)
Total Recipe Amount: 10 oz (283.5 g)

INGREDIENTS

- 1 cup cooked salmon, chopped
- 1 cup oat flour
- 1 egg

Prep. time: 15 min   Cook time: 30 min

DIRECTIONS

1. Preheat your oven to 350°F (175°C).
2. Combine the chopped salmon, oat flour, and egg in a mixing bowl. Mix until well combined.
3. Roll the mixture into bite-sized balls and place them on a baking sheet lined with parchment paper.
4. Bake for 30 minutes or until the bites are firm and slightly golden. Allow to cool before serving.

DUCK TRAINING TREATS

28% protein, 32% carbohydrates, 15% fat, 10% minerals, 7% fiber, 5% cholesterol, 2% sodium, 1% potassium
Total Calories: 370 kcal (1.30 kcal/g, 37.0 kcal/oz)
Total Recipe Amount: 10 oz (283.5 g)

INGREDIENTS

- 1 cup cooked duck, chopped
- 1 cup oat flour
- 1 egg

Prep. time: 15 min   Cook time: 30 min

DIRECTIONS

1. Preheat your oven to 350°F (175°C).
2. Combine the chopped duck, oat flour, and egg in a mixing bowl. Mix until well combined.
3. Roll the mixture into bite-sized balls and place them on a baking sheet lined with parchment paper.
4. Bake for 30 minutes or until the treats are firm and slightly golden. Allow to cool before serving.

LAMB TRAINING BITES

26% protein, 34% carbohydrates, 14% fat, 8% minerals, 6% fiber, 4% cholesterol, 5% sodium, 3% potassium
Total Calories: 350 kcal (1.24 kcal/g, 35.1 kcal/oz)
Total Recipe Amount: 10 oz (283.5 g)

INGREDIENTS

- 1 cup cooked lamb, chopped
- 1 cup oat flour
- 1 egg

Prep. time: 15 min   Cook time: 30 min

DIRECTIONS

1. Preheat your oven to 350°F (175°C).
2. Combine the chopped lamb, oat flour, and egg in a mixing bowl. Mix until well combined.
3. Roll the mixture into bite-sized balls and place them on a baking sheet lined with parchment paper.
4. Bake for 30 minutes or until the bites are firm and slightly golden. Allow to cool before serving.

VENISON TRAINING TREATS

28% protein, 32% carbohydrates, 15% fat, 10% minerals, 7% fiber, 5% cholesterol, 2% sodium, 1% potassium
Total Calories: 370 kcal (1.30 kcal/g, 37.0 kcal/oz)
Total Recipe Amount: 10 oz (283.5 g)

INGREDIENTS

- 1 cup cooked venison, chopped
- 1 cup oat flour
- 1 egg

Prep. time: 15 min   Cook time: 30 min

DIRECTIONS

1. Preheat your oven to 350°F (175°C).
2. Combine the chopped venison, oat flour, and egg in a mixing bowl. Mix until well combined.
3. Roll the mixture into bite-sized balls and place them on a baking sheet lined with parchment paper.
4. Bake for 30 minutes or until the treats are firm and slightly golden. Allow to cool before serving.

PEANUT BUTTER TRAINING BITES

25% protein, 35% carbohydrates, 12% fat, 10% minerals, 7% fiber, 5% cholesterol, 3% sodium, 3% potassium
Total Calories: 340 kcal (1.20 kcal/g, 34.0 kcal/oz)
Total Recipe Amount: 10 oz (283.5 g)

INGREDIENTS

- 1 cup peanut butter (unsalted, xylitol-free)
- 1 cup oat flour
- 1 egg

Prep. time: 15 min   Cook time: 30 min

DIRECTIONS

1. Preheat your oven to 350°F (175°C).
2. Combine the peanut butter, oat flour, and egg in a mixing bowl. Mix until well combined.
3. Roll the mixture into bite-sized balls and place them on a baking sheet lined with parchment paper.
4. Bake for 30 minutes or until the bites are firm and slightly golden. Allow to cool before serving.

CHEESE TRAINING TREATS

24% protein, 36% carbohydrates, 12% fat, 8% minerals, 6% fiber, 5% cholesterol, 5% sodium, 4% potassium
Total Calories: 330 kcal (1.16 kcal/g, 33.0 kcal/oz)
Total Recipe Amount: 10 oz (283.5 g)

INGREDIENTS

- 1 cup grated cheese
- 1 cup oat flour
- 1 egg

Prep. time: 15 min   Cook time: 30 min

DIRECTIONS

1. Preheat your oven to 350°F (175°C).
2. Combine the grated cheese, oat flour, and egg in a mixing bowl. Mix until well combined.
3. Roll the mixture into bite-sized balls and place them on a baking sheet lined with parchment paper.
4. Bake for 30 minutes or until the treats are firm and slightly golden. Allow to cool before serving.

SUPPLEMENTS AND ADDITIONS

FISH OIL SUPPLEMENT

0% protein, 0% carbohydrates, 100% fat, 0% minerals, 0% fiber, 0% cholesterol, 0% sodium, 0% potassium
Total Calories: 892 kcal (8.92 kcal/g, 254.8 kcal/oz)
Total Recipe Amount: 3.5 oz (100 g)

INGREDIENTS

- 2 lbs of fresh, oily fish (such as mackerel, salmon, or sardines)
- 1 cup water

| Prep. time: 20 min | Cook time: 30 min |

DIRECTIONS

1. Clean and fillet the fish, leaving the skin on.
2. Place fillets in a pot with 1 cup of water. Simmer over medium heat until soft and breaking apart, about 20-30 minutes.
3. Cool slightly, then strain through cheesecloth, pressing gently to extract the oil.
4. Refrigerate the liquid overnight. Scoop the solidified oil from the top into a clean container.
5. Store in an airtight container in the refrigerator for up to a week, or freeze for longer storage.

BONE BROTH ADDITION

2% protein, 0% carbohydrates, 1% fat, 3% minerals, 0% fiber, 0% cholesterol, 0% sodium, 0% potassium
Total Calories: 0 kcal (0 kcal/g, 0 kcal/oz)
Total Recipe Amount: 128 oz (3629 g)

INGREDIENTS

- 2 pounds beef bones
- 1 gallon water
- 2 tbsp apple cider vinegar (or lemon juice)

| Prep. time: 15 min | Cook time: 480 min |

DIRECTIONS

1. Place the beef bones in a large pot.
2. Add the water and apple cider vinegar (or lemon juice).
3. Bring to a boil, then reduce heat and simmer for 8 hours.
4. Strain the broth, discard the bones, and let it cool.
5. Store in the refrigerator and add to your dog's food as needed.

HOMEMADE GLUCOSAMINE BROTH

0% protein, 0% carbohydrates, 0% fat, 0% minerals, 0% fiber, 0% cholesterol, 0% sodium, 0% potassium
Total Calories: 0 kcal (0 kcal/g, 0 kcal/oz)
Total Recipe Amount: 128 oz (3629 g)

INGREDIENTS

- 2 lbs fresh chicken feet
- 1 gallon water
- 2 tbsp apple cider vinegar

Prep. time: 30 min   Cook time: 300 min

DIRECTIONS

1. Rinse chicken feet under cold water, removing any dirt or skin.
2. Place chicken feet in a large pot with water and apple cider vinegar.
3. Bring to a boil, then simmer for 4-5 hours until the feet are very soft and the broth is gelatinous.
4. Remove feet and let broth cool slightly. Strain to remove solid particles.
5. Pour broth into ice cube trays and freeze. Transfer frozen cubes to a freezer-safe bag or container for easy use.

TURMERIC PASTE

2% protein, 4% carbohydrates, 10% fat, 1% minerals, 3% fiber, 0% cholesterol, 2% sodium, 1% potassium
Total Calories: 90 kcal (0.54 kcal/g, 15.3 kcal/oz)
Total Recipe Amount: 6 oz (170 g)

INGREDIENTS

- 1/4 cup turmeric powder
- 1/2 cup water
- 1 1/2 tsp ground black pepper
- 1/4 cup coconut oil

Prep. time: 5 min   Cook time: 10 min

DIRECTIONS

1. Combine the turmeric powder and water in a small saucepan. Stir over low heat until a thick paste forms (about 7-10 minutes). Add more water if needed.
2. Once the paste is thick and smooth, remove from heat and stir in the ground black pepper and coconut oil until well combined.
3. Allow the mixture to cool, then transfer it to a clean jar with a tight-fitting lid.
4. Store the turmeric paste in the refrigerator for up to 2 weeks.

CALCIUM SUPPLEMENT WITH CRUSHED EGGSHELLS

0% protein, 0% carbohydrates, 0% fat, 99% minerals, 0% fiber, 0% cholesterol, 0% sodium, 1% potassium
Total Calories: 0 kcal (0 kcal/g, 0 kcal/oz)
Total Recipe Amount: 1 oz (28 g)

INGREDIENTS

- 10 eggshells

Prep. time: 5 min	Cook time: 15 min

DIRECTIONS

1. Preheat your oven to 350°F (175°C).
2. Clean and dry the eggshells thoroughly.
3. Place the eggshells on a baking sheet and bake for 15 minutes.
4. Cool, then grind into a fine powder using a food processor.
5. Store in an airtight container and add a small amount to your dog's food as needed.

HOMEMADE PROBIOTICS FOR DOGS

0% protein, 5% carbohydrates, 0% fat, 5% minerals, 0% fiber, 0% cholesterol, 0% sodium, 5% potassium
Total Calories: 50 kcal (0.42 kcal/g, 11.9 kcal/oz)
Total Recipe Amount: 10.5 oz (300 g)

INGREDIENTS

- 1 cup plain, unsweetened yogurt
- 1 tbsp ground flaxseed
- 1 tbsp raw honey
- 1 ripe banana, mashed

Prep. time: 10 min	Cook time: 0 min

DIRECTIONS

1. Combine the yogurt, ground flaxseed, raw honey, and mashed banana in a mixing bowl.
2. Stir the mixture until all ingredients are well combined.
3. Divide the mixture into silicone molds or ice cube trays.
4. Freeze for at least 2 hours or until solid. Store in the freezer for up to 2 months.

DRINKS

NON-ALCOHOLIC DOG BEER

4% protein, 2% carbohydrates, 0% fat, 1% minerals, 0% fiber, 0% cholesterol, 90% sodium, 3% potassium
Total Calories: 103 kcal (0.14 kcal/g, 3.96 kcal/oz)
Total Recipe Amount: 26 oz (737 g)

INGREDIENTS

- 2 cups beef broth
- 1 cup water
- 1/4 cup unsweetened apple juice

Prep. time: 10 min   Cook time: 20 min

DIRECTIONS

1. Bring the beef broth, water, and apple juice to a simmer in a pot.
2. Let it cool completely before serving it to your dog.
3. Pour the mixture into a bowl or bottle for your dog to enjoy.

CHICKEN BROTH DOG DRINK

3% protein, 0% carbohydrates, 0% fat, 2% minerals, 0% fiber, 0% cholesterol, 92% sodium, 3% potassium
Total Calories: 72 kcal (0.10 kcal/g, 3.0 kcal/oz)
Total Recipe Amount: 24 oz (680.3 g)

INGREDIENTS

- 2 cups chicken broth
- 1 cup water

Prep. time: 10 min   Cook time: 20 min

DIRECTIONS

1. Bring the chicken broth and water to a simmer in a pot.
2. Let it cool completely before serving it to your dog.
3. Pour the mixture into a bowl or bottle for your dog to enjoy.

TURKEY AND CRANBERRY DOG DRINK

5% protein, 5% carbohydrates, 0% fat, 2% minerals, 2% fiber, 0% cholesterol, 85% sodium, 1% potassium
Total Calories: 117.9 kcal (0.16 kcal/g, 4.5 kcal/oz)
Total Recipe Amount: 26 oz (737 g)

INGREDIENTS

- 2 cups turkey broth
- 1/4 cup cranberries, chopped
- 1 cup water

Prep. time: 10 min   Cook time: 20 min

DIRECTIONS

1. Bring the turkey broth, chopped cranberries, and water to a simmer in a pot.
2. Let it cool completely before serving it to your dog.
3. Pour the mixture into a bowl or bottle for your dog to enjoy.

PUMPKIN AND APPLE SMOOTHIE

2% protein, 70% carbohydrates, 2% fat, 5% minerals, 8% fiber, 0% cholesterol, 1% sodium, 12% potassium
Total Calories: 178.5 kcal (0.42 kcal/g, 11.9 kcal/oz)
Total Recipe Amount: 15 oz (425 g)

INGREDIENTS

- 1/2 cup pumpkin puree
- 1/2 cup apple, chopped
- 1 cup water

Prep. time: 10 min   Cook time: 0 min

DIRECTIONS

1. Bring the chicken broth and water to a simmer in a pot.
2. Let it cool completely before serving it to your dog.
3. Pour the mixture into a bowl or bottle for your dog to enjoy.

BLUEBERRY AND SPINACH SMOOTHIE

4% protein, 65% carbohydrates, 3% fat, 8% minerals, 10% fiber, 0% cholesterol, 1% sodium, 9% potassium
Total Calories: 154 kcal (0.39 kcal/g, 11.0 kcal/oz)
Total Recipe Amount: 14 oz (395 g)

INGREDIENTS

- 1/2 cup blueberries
- 1/2 cup fresh spinach
- 1 cup water

Prep. time: 10 min	Cook time: 0 min

DIRECTIONS

1. Combine the blueberries, spinach, and water in a blender. Blend until smooth.
2. Pour the mixture into a bowl or bottle for your dog to enjoy.

CARROT AND GINGER DOG DRINK

2% protein, 70% carbohydrates, 1% fat, 7% minerals, 8% fiber, 0% cholesterol, 2% sodium, 10% potassium
Total Calories: 120 kcal (0.35 kcal/g, 10.0 kcal/oz)
Total Recipe Amount: 12 oz (340 g)

INGREDIENTS

- 1/2 cup carrots, chopped
- 1/2 tsp fresh ginger, grated
- 1 cup water

Prep. time: 10 min	Cook time: 0 min

DIRECTIONS

1. Combine the chopped carrots, grated ginger, and water in a blender. Blend until smooth.
2. Pour the mixture into a bowl or bottle for your dog to enjoy.

SWEET POTATO AND BANANA SMOOTHIE

3% protein, 75% carbohydrates, 2% fat, 5% minerals, 8% fiber, 0% cholesterol, 1% sodium, 6% potassium
Total Calories: 180 kcal (0.45 kcal/g, 12.85 kcal/oz)
Total Recipe Amount: 14 oz (395 g)

INGREDIENTS

- 1/2 cup cooked sweet potato, mashed
- 1/2 banana, mashed
- 1 cup water

Prep. time: 10 min   Cook time: 0 min

DIRECTIONS

1. Combine the mashed sweet potato, mashed banana, and water in a blender. Blend until smooth.
2. Pour the mixture into a bowl or bottle for your dog to enjoy.

MINT AND CUCUMBER DOG WATER

0% protein, 5% carbohydrates, 0% fat, 3% minerals, 1% fiber, 0% cholesterol, 1% sodium, 90% potassium
Total Calories: 18 kcal (0.05 kcal/g, 1.5 kcal/oz)
Total Recipe Amount: 12 oz (340 g)

INGREDIENTS

- 1/2 cup cucumber, chopped
- 1 tbsp fresh mint, chopped
- 1 cup water

Prep. time: 10 min   Cook time: 0 min

DIRECTIONS

1. Combine the chopped cucumber, fresh mint, and water in a blender. Blend until smooth.
2. Pour the mixture into a bowl or bottle for your dog to enjoy.

BERRY AND COCONUT WATER DOG DRINK

1% protein, 50% carbohydrates, 3% fat, 5% minerals, 8% fiber, 0% cholesterol, 1% sodium, 32% potassium
Total Calories: 109 kcal (0.32 kcal/g, 9.1 kcal/oz)
Total Recipe Amount: 12 oz (340 g)

INGREDIENTS

- 1/2 cup mixed berries (blueberries, strawberries, raspberries)
- 1 cup coconut water

Prep. time: 10 min	Cook time: 0 min

DIRECTIONS

1. Combine the mixed berries and coconut water in a blender. Blend until smooth.
2. Pour the mixture into a bowl or bottle for your dog to enjoy.

WATERMELON AND MINT DOG DRINK

1% protein, 80% carbohydrates, 0% fat, 3% minerals, 5% fiber, 0% cholesterol, 1% sodium, 10% potassium
Total Calories: 97.6 kcal (0.21 kcal/g, 6.1 kcal/oz)
Total Recipe Amount: 16 oz (460 g)

INGREDIENTS

- 1 cup watermelon, chopped
- 1 tbsp fresh mint, chopped
- 1 cup water

Prep. time: 10 min	Cook time: 0 min

DIRECTIONS

1. Combine the chopped watermelon, fresh mint, and water in a blender. Blend until smooth.
2. Pour the mixture into a bowl or bottle for your dog to enjoy.

RECIPE INDEX

Oats

NOTES

RECIPE NAME	DIFFICULTY	RATING
	① ② ③ ④ ⑤	☆ ☆ ☆ ☆ ☆
	① ② ③ ④ ⑤	☆ ☆ ☆ ☆ ☆
	① ② ③ ④ ⑤	☆ ☆ ☆ ☆ ☆
	① ② ③ ④ ⑤	☆ ☆ ☆ ☆ ☆
	① ② ③ ④ ⑤	☆ ☆ ☆ ☆ ☆
	① ② ③ ④ ⑤	☆ ☆ ☆ ☆ ☆
	① ② ③ ④ ⑤	☆ ☆ ☆ ☆ ☆
	① ② ③ ④ ⑤	☆ ☆ ☆ ☆ ☆
	① ② ③ ④ ⑤	☆ ☆ ☆ ☆ ☆
	① ② ③ ④ ⑤	☆ ☆ ☆ ☆ ☆
	① ② ③ ④ ⑤	☆ ☆ ☆ ☆ ☆
	① ② ③ ④ ⑤	☆ ☆ ☆ ☆ ☆
	① ② ③ ④ ⑤	☆ ☆ ☆ ☆ ☆
	① ② ③ ④ ⑤	☆ ☆ ☆ ☆ ☆
	① ② ③ ④ ⑤	☆ ☆ ☆ ☆ ☆
	① ② ③ ④ ⑤	☆ ☆ ☆ ☆ ☆
	① ② ③ ④ ⑤	☆ ☆ ☆ ☆ ☆
	① ② ③ ④ ⑤	☆ ☆ ☆ ☆ ☆
	① ② ③ ④ ⑤	☆ ☆ ☆ ☆ ☆

NOTES

RECIPE NAME	DIFFICULTY	RATING
	① ② ③ ④ ⑤	☆ ☆ ☆ ☆ ☆
	① ② ③ ④ ⑤	☆ ☆ ☆ ☆ ☆
	① ② ③ ④ ⑤	☆ ☆ ☆ ☆ ☆
	① ② ③ ④ ⑤	☆ ☆ ☆ ☆ ☆
	① ② ③ ④ ⑤	☆ ☆ ☆ ☆ ☆
	① ② ③ ④ ⑤	☆ ☆ ☆ ☆ ☆
	① ② ③ ④ ⑤	☆ ☆ ☆ ☆ ☆
	① ② ③ ④ ⑤	☆ ☆ ☆ ☆ ☆
	① ② ③ ④ ⑤	☆ ☆ ☆ ☆ ☆
	① ② ③ ④ ⑤	☆ ☆ ☆ ☆ ☆
	① ② ③ ④ ⑤	☆ ☆ ☆ ☆ ☆
	① ② ③ ④ ⑤	☆ ☆ ☆ ☆ ☆
	① ② ③ ④ ⑤	☆ ☆ ☆ ☆ ☆
	① ② ③ ④ ⑤	☆ ☆ ☆ ☆ ☆
	① ② ③ ④ ⑤	☆ ☆ ☆ ☆ ☆
	① ② ③ ④ ⑤	☆ ☆ ☆ ☆ ☆
	① ② ③ ④ ⑤	☆ ☆ ☆ ☆ ☆
	① ② ③ ④ ⑤	☆ ☆ ☆ ☆ ☆

NOTES

RECIPE NAME	DIFFICULTY	RATING
	① ② ③ ④ ⑤	☆ ☆ ☆ ☆ ☆
	① ② ③ ④ ⑤	☆ ☆ ☆ ☆ ☆
	① ② ③ ④ ⑤	☆ ☆ ☆ ☆ ☆
	① ② ③ ④ ⑤	☆ ☆ ☆ ☆ ☆
	① ② ③ ④ ⑤	☆ ☆ ☆ ☆ ☆
	① ② ③ ④ ⑤	☆ ☆ ☆ ☆ ☆
	① ② ③ ④ ⑤	☆ ☆ ☆ ☆ ☆
	① ② ③ ④ ⑤	☆ ☆ ☆ ☆ ☆
	① ② ③ ④ ⑤	☆ ☆ ☆ ☆ ☆
	① ② ③ ④ ⑤	☆ ☆ ☆ ☆ ☆
	① ② ③ ④ ⑤	☆ ☆ ☆ ☆ ☆
	① ② ③ ④ ⑤	☆ ☆ ☆ ☆ ☆
	① ② ③ ④ ⑤	☆ ☆ ☆ ☆ ☆
	① ② ③ ④ ⑤	☆ ☆ ☆ ☆ ☆
	① ② ③ ④ ⑤	☆ ☆ ☆ ☆ ☆
	① ② ③ ④ ⑤	☆ ☆ ☆ ☆ ☆
	① ② ③ ④ ⑤	☆ ☆ ☆ ☆ ☆
	① ② ③ ④ ⑤	☆ ☆ ☆ ☆ ☆

BONUS!

I hope you and your furry friend enjoy the Homemade Healthy Dog Food Cookbook. But before you close this book, pick up your gift!

Please scan the QR code to get the Bonus Book. It's a 30-page PDF where you'll find:

- **An additional chapter, "Food Allergies in Dogs," with the Dog Food Allergy Chart to help identify and manage common food allergies in your furry family members.**

- **Color pictures of the recipes from the main book (Baked, No-Bake, Slow-Cooked, Frozen, Special Diets, and Holiday Treats).**

- **Eight extra recipes from the seasonal collection with color pictures to keep your dog's diet varied and engaging throughout the year.**

Thank you for being a part of our community and choosing to nourish your dog with love and care!

Made in the USA
Las Vegas, NV
04 November 2024

11096967R00085